THE LIBRARY
ST. MARY'S COLLEGE OF MARYLAND
ST. MARY'S CITY, MARYLAND 20686

085228

D1803869

TWAYNE'S WORLD AUTHORS SERIES
A Survey of the World's Literature

MEXICO

Luis Davila, Indiana University
EDITOR

Heriberto Frías

TWAS 486

Heriberto Frías

HERIBERTO FRÍAS

By JAMES W. BROWN
Ball State University

TWAYNE PUBLISHERS
A DIVISION OF G. K. HALL & CO., BOSTON

Copyright © 1978 by G. K. Hall & Co.
All Rights Reserved
First Printing

Library of Congress Cataloging in Publication Data

Brown, James W 1934–
  Heriberto Frías.

  (Twayne's world authors series ; TWAS 486 : Mexico)
  Bibliography: p. 132–33
  Includes index.
  1. Frías, Heriberto, 1870–1925—Criticism and interpretation. I. Title.
PQ7297.F75Z63   863   77-16234
ISBN O-8057-6327-9

MANUFACTURED IN THE UNITED STATES OF AMERICA

Contents

About the Author
Preface
Acknowledgments
Chronology
1. Frías' Life and Times 13
2. *Tomochic* 38
3. The Other Novels 55
4. Other Works of Frías 75
5. Some Observations: Four Keys to Frías 100
   Notes and References 125
   Selected Bibliography 133
   Index 135

About the Author

James W. Brown is Professor of Foreign Languages at Ball State University. He received his Ph.D. at Indiana University in 1967 and has published a critical edition of *Tomochic* (Mexico City: Porrúa, 1968), and articles and reviews in *El Nacional, Hispania, Contemporary Latin America, Boletín Bibliográfico, Symposium, Modern Language Journal, Foreign Language Annals, Nueva Narrativa Hispanoamericana,* and *Essays in Literature.* He is married and has three children.

Preface

Heriberto Frías has been one of the most underestimated figures in Mexican literary history. Adequate recognition of his importance has been long in coming, even though in retrospect it can be shown that he was a literary gadfly of the Días regime and a harbinger, not only of the coming Revolution, but also of the "literature of the Revolution" as later exemplified by Mariano Azuela and others. In style and content, Frías' *Tomochic* foreshadows the Novel of the Revolution in a number of important ways, while ¿*Aguila o sol?* is a curious and disquieting example of that cycle. His works in general anticipate much of what has happened later in the twentieth century novel, and many of them, particularly the satirical pieces, can also be read with pleasure for their lively evocation of Mexico's past and for the rich, popular Mexican language that Frías boldly cultivated while his contemporaries were still copying European elegance. Frías combined this unabashed popular flavor with strong Naturalist influence to produce works that look deeply into Mexico's soul and do not like all that they see.

It is no cliché to say that Frías' life, in great measure, *was* his work. In fact, the protagonists of his novels are himself in thin disguise, and his own rebellious and disorderly life forms the very fabric of many of his writings. Still, his life, except for a few well-publicized episodes, has not been carefully detailed by critics, so the present study will give somewhat more than the usual recounting of his biography. And too, since Frías' profession was journalism, this study will sample his journalistic pieces, thus showing how Frías reacted to his social, literary, and ideological surroundings—for example, the Positivist dogma that dominated Mexican social thought at the time.

Frías' life and works, taken together show one man's journey through a most difficult and trying time. Even his childhood was characterized by the vertiginous rises and dips of fortune that continued throughout his life. Later, as a young army officer, he came face to face with the raw cruelty of Mexico's dictatorship and at the same time, almost by accident, became a writer, a national figure, and very nearly a martyr in the cause of freedom with his publication of *Tomochic*. Then, as though shoved into the limelight with no song to sing, Frías spent the next years finding his way as an author and an anti-Díaz critic. In neither case was his route a straight or sure one; there were reverses in both. But all the while, Frías sought to understand Mexico and to denounce the ills that were plaguing it in such writings as *El amor de las sirenas (The Love of the Sirens)* and *El triunfo de Sancho Panza (The Triumph of Sancho Panza)*, as well as many others.

As the new century got underway, Frías was among the first to take up the banner of Madero in resisting the dictatorship. Like Madero, he preferred peaceful democratic change, but he became a revolutionary when forced to do so, and as the Madero revolt briefly triumphed, Frías' fortunes first boosted him into select governmental circles, then into hiding as Huerta usurped the presidency and murdered Madero. Later, Frías' support of Villa earned him the animosity of Carranza, and once again Frías nearly lost his life and was forced into retirement until Obregón's presidency. Throughout all this, Frías' writings continued to look mostly back on prerevolutionary Mexico, although he made two efforts to write his story of the revolution, as we shall see.

This study will center around an ordering and a description of Frías' works in their varied forms and evolution through his tumultuous career. Following an examination of Frías' life and times, the novels are taken up first because Frías is best known as a novelist. Due to the multiple problems surrounding *Tomochic*, a separate chapter is devoted to that novel; then the others are examined in chronological order. His "other works" are divided into historical works, contemporary satire and short stories, poetry and drama. As stated before, his editorial pieces will be presented in the biography instead of separately, though this by no means implies that they are less "literary," for like Lizardi, the first Mexican novelist, much of his talent was invested in daily skirmishes with the printing press.

The reader who wishes to delve further into Frías' works will unfortunately soon find that many are now quite rare; this is a lack that perhaps time and reediting may hopefully change.

JAMES W. BROWN

Ball State University

Acknowledgments

I extend my sincere thanks to Dr. Merle E. Simmons of the Department of Spanish and Portuguese at Indiana University for guiding me in my initial study of Heriberto Frías a few years ago; to José Valadés, Andrés Magallón, and Porfirio Martínez Peñalosa for their invaluable information regarding Frías; and posthumously to Sra. Aurea Delgado de Frías for her generous and kindly chats and letters about her late husband. My gratitude also goes to José Antonio Pérez Porrúa of Ediciones Porrúa for permission to quote from my 1968 edition of Frías' *Tomochic;* to Donald W. Bleznick, editor of *Hispania,* for permission to use material from my article "Heriberto Frías: A Mexican Zola"; to Pamela Blanco, who typed and found misspellings, and to the Department of Foreign Languages of Ball State University for providing her services; to Luis Dávila of the Department of Spanish and Portuguese at Indiana University for his careful and thoughtful reading of the manuscript; and to my wife, Phyllis, for her aid in more ways than she imagines.

Chronology

1870 Heriberto Frías born in Querétaro, May 15, son of Antonio Frías and Dolores Alcocer.
1882 Frías family moves to Mexico City.
1887 Enters Colegio Militar.
1889 Leaves Colegio Militar; enters army; jailed twice.
1892 Participates in the Tomochic campaign.
1893 First edition of *Tomochic* published in *El Demócrata*, March 14–April 14; Frías jailed and tried, then cashiered from the army.
1894 In Mexico City, works on the newspaper staff of *Gil Blas*; second edition of *Tomochic* published.
1895 Writes on staff of *El Demócrata*; publishes *Naufragio (Derelict)*, a novel denouncing the vices of Mexico City life; is jailed. Verástegui-Romero duel occurs in Mexico City.
1896 Publishes *El último duelo (The Last Duel)*, based on Verástegui-Romero duel; works on newspaper *El Combate*.
1899 Third edition of *Tomochic*; *Leyendas históricas mexicanas (Mexican Historical Legends)* published in book form; marries Antonia Figueroa.
1900 *Biblioteca del niño mexicano (Books for Mexican Children)*, children's booklets popularizing Mexican history.
1901 *Episodios militares mexicanos (Mexican Military Episodes)*.
1903 Tries unsuccessfully to reenter army.
1906 Arrives in Mazatlán as editor of *El Correo de la Tarde*; fourth edition of *Tomochic*.
1907 Second edition of *El último duelo (The Last Duel)*.
1908 *El amor de las sirenas (The Love of Sirens)*, revision of *Naufragio (Derelict)*.
1909 Leads Maderist campaign to elect José Ferrel as governor of Sinaloa; expeled when Ferrel loses; returns to Mexico City as editor of *El Progreso Latino* and works for the statesman Francisco I. Madero.
1910 Antonia, his wife, dies; Madero's revolt occurs; marries Aurea Delgado; Frías escapes to the north.

1911   Fifth edition of *Tomochic; El triunfo de Sancho Panza (The Triumph of Sancho Panza)*, a novel based on his experiences in Mazatlán; named to Madero's revolutionary party reorganization commission; appointed undersecretary of foreign affairs; returns to Mazatlán as government fiscal chief.

1913   Victoriano Huerta's counterrevolt against Madero; Frías flees north.

1914   Joins Aguascalientes Constitutional Convention as editor of *La Convención*.

1915   Edits both *La Convención* and *El Monitor* as the Constitutional Convention continues; works on *El diluvio en México (The Mexican Deluge)*, a novel about the revolution, since lost; *Los piratas del boulevard (The Pirates of the Boulevard)*, collection of satires previously published in newspapers.

1916   *Miserias de México (Miseries of Mexico)*, which describes Frías' young years as a journalist; as Venustiano Carranza defeats Conventionists, Frías is jailed, sentenced to death, and later released; under pressure from Carranza, Frías retires from public life.

1918   *La vida de Juan Soldado (The Life of Juan the Soldier)*, a tribute to Mexican soldiers.

1920   Carranza killed; Alvaro Obregón becomes president.

1921   Named Mexican Consul to Cádiz, Spain; *Leyendas históricas mexicanas por Heriberto Frías (Mexican Historical Legends by Heriberto Frías)*, edited in New York by James Bardin.

1923   Returns to Mexico via Paris; publishes *¿Aguila o sol? (Heads or Tails?)*, first of a trilogy about the revolution.

1924   Teaches Mexican history at the National Military School.

1925   *Album histórico popular de la Ciudad de México (Popular Historical Album of Mexico City)*, a popularized history of Mexico City co-authored with Rafael Martínez; Frías dies on November 12.

1955   *Episodios militares mexicanos (Mexican Military Episodes)* republished in facsimile.

1960   *Tomochic* republished in facsimile.

1965   *Leyendas históricas mexicanas (Mexican Historical Legends)* republished in facsimile.

1968   *Tomochic* edited with prologue by James W. Brown.

CHAPTER 1

Frías' Life and Times

Heriberto Frías, a valiant and honorable officer, a noble thinker and writer, angered by the stupidity of his superior officers and the infamies that they made him commit in bringing him to exterminate his brothers, wrote a very excellent book denouncing those outrages. But the manly voice of men of heart is never pleasing to despots who rule over the land, and that honorable officer was discharged, brought to trial and very nearly went before the firing-squad.[1]

WITH these words Francisco Madero, the "Apostle of the Mexican Revolution," paid tribute to his follower and companion-at-arms, Heriberto Frías. It had been in 1893 that the "very excellent book" that Madero mentioned, *Tomochic*, appeared and set off a series of events that changed the young soldier-poet into a combative journalist and author. Thus transformed, Frías devoted his life to producing a profusion of works, painting in bold colors the ragged underside of his society and the injustices of the Porfirio Díaz dictatorship (1877–1880 and 1884–1910). In return, he was ostracized and persecuted as no other Mexican writer since Fernández de Lizardi of the times of independence. It was the Díaz era that provided the raw material for Frías' works; even after the gaudy, top-heavy regime fell in 1910, most of his writings were to look back to the days when Porfirio Díaz ruled Mexico.

To understand better the life and writings of Heriberto Frías, we should review briefly the Díaz period's social and cultural climate in order to make clearer in later chapters how deeply those years influenced his writings. For this purpose we shall return to the beginning years of the Díaz era.

I *Porfirio Díaz and his Positivist Paradise*

In Mexico, the 1870s began with great promise but ended with the ironclad dictatorship of Porfirio Díaz. Benito Juárez, Mexico's great liberal president, had died unexpectedly in 1872, leaving his successor, Sebastián Lerdo de Tejada, with the overwhelming problems of a young government, including that of an empty treasury. Lerdo proved to be a disappointment. During his term of office, he steadily lost what popularity he had enjoyed as Juárez' unsuccessful opponent in the 1871 election, so that when he defeated Díaz in the election of 1876, it was only because he controlled the government machinery. The outbreak of chaos and revolts generated by this fraudulent election provided an opportunity for Díaz, an ex-general turned sugar-grower and revolutionary, to proclaim his *Plan de Tuxtepec* (Declaration at Tuxtepec), raise troops, and defeat the government's forces after a few months of fighting.[2]

In ascending to the presidency, Díaz rode the crest of a new optimism in Mexico. During the decade following the period of French intervention (1864–1867), momentum had already grown in favor of Mexico's joining the community of rich and stylish societies led by Western Europe and the United States. Mexico's leading citizens saw, for themselves at least, a shining future of railroads, telegraph lines, mines, factories, wealth, and luxury.[3]

These were also days of a new faith: science. The nineteenth century had produced such a wealth of discoveries and innovations that Western man tended to feel himself on the brink of a new era in which science would satisfy all of man's needs, settle his differences, and compensate for his faults. To this end, Días inherited from Juárez and Lerdo a state philosophy ready made and suited to his purposes. This philosophy was August Comte's doctrine of Positivism, which had molded Mexico's public educational system since its official adoption in 1867 by Juárez' minister of education, Gabino Barreda.[4] Briefly stated, Comte's philosophy placed scientific knowledge acquired by observation and classification of tangible data above all other forms of knowledge, such as that gained by pure reason, intuition, or faith. It further held that the scientific method could be applied to the social as well as the natural sciences. This led to a new view of society.

In the perfect society envisioned by Comte, all men would rationally recognize their rightful place in accordance with their talents and abilities. Some would lead, others would follow, and fruitful stability would result. Mexico's leading citizens, particularly the expanding middle class, eagerly embraced the prospects of such a society. Seeking to moderate the rebellious liberalism that had characterized much of the middle class in previous decades, Barreda (with Juárez' blessings) was given the task of ushering the new ideology through the door of public education. And so Positivism became Mexico's official doctrine and guiding light.[5]

Comte's philosophy, zealously applied, brought changes to Mexico's educational system. With Positivism for their weapon, the anticlerical liberals of Juárez' administration wrested the public schools from the church and forbade the teaching of religion in classrooms. The new system, and its central institution, the National Preparatory School, stressed the scientific attitude in all matters and fostered empirical knowledge, free investigation, and practical application. Cutting deeply into traditional Latin verbosity and hollow rhetoric, the schools brought forth a generation of clear-thinking and practical leaders dedicated to progress and material well-being. But when Díaz came to power, Juárez' other ideals of liberty and democracy were shoved aside, victims of the ensuing scramble for economic advantage, and Positivism became a national cult which regarded with indulgence oppression and pillage in the name of order and progress.[6]

By a skillful juggling of Positivist-oriented ideas, Díaz succeeded in maintaining for three decades the general support of Mexico's intelligentsia and opinion-makers. He gave them governmental and educational positions, made sure that favorable newspapers prospered, and even tolerated an occasional and limited amount of criticism from them. His supporters continued in his camp, not only because it was to their benefit, but also because they feared that only the *Caudillo* (strongman) stood between them and a return to revolt and anarchy. They believed that the restrictions on liberty that he imposed, such as control of the courts and the press, were merely temporary and would be removed as soon as conditions were to permit. Thus, as Díaz settled firmly into his role as "perpetual president," business interests, landholders, the church, and the growing legions of foreign investors found it profitable to remain on good terms with him.

A final blow to the old liberalism came in 1893, when José Ives Limantour became minister of the treasury. A wealthy young financier of French extraction, Limantour brought with him a clique of lawyers and intellectuals, most of them educated at the National Preparatory School. They could be called second generation Positivists, for they were products of the new school system where they had studied the thought of latter-day European Positivists such as John Stuart Mill and Herbert Spencer. Consequently, Limantour and his associates entered high finance and government with the attitude that a state could and should be scientifically managed; hence they were popularly called the *científicos* (scientists).

This group of men, representatives of Mexico's new aristocracy, came to exert an influence in their country's affairs second only to that of the dictator himself. They energetically put into practice the teachings of Spencer, a Social Darwinist who had applied evolutionary theory to the newborn social sciences. In Europe, the business and economic world had already embraced Spencer's philosophy reduced to its rawest terms; there it had become a widespread belief in a social "survival of the fittest," whereby the wealthy and powerful considered themselves "fit" by virtue of their wealth and power, and those less fortunate were therefore deemed "inferior." All moral considerations were consequently brushed aside, and the result was unrestricted economic warfare. This also was the new Positivism known and practiced by the *científicos*, as it was easily incorporated into existing governmental policy. In the hands of the *científicos*, these self-serving ideas rose to doctrinal proportions. Mexico prospered as a utilitarian place of business, subject only to the rule of profit and loss. Such was the rampant materialism that a newspaper published a burlesque Positivist credo that began: "I believe in the Almighty Ounce of Gold, Creator of all good and evil, and in the Banknote, Its only child. . . ."[7]

It seemed to many that the prophecies of a new era were near fulfillment, as roads, railways, and industries grew, and Mexico City blossomed into a showplace of theaters, ballrooms, parks, and boulevards for the amusement of refined ladies and elegant gentlemen. But in drastic contrast to the well-being of the upper crust, the Mexican masses, largely Indian, lived in deplorable poverty, plagued by disease, ignorance, and persecution.[8] They were viewed as a resource, like property or mineral rights, to be used and expended at will.[9] To these masses the Díaz government signified only repression. Poorly clothed, badly fed, and totally unlettered, the lower classes led a brutish life, lightened only by quantities of cheap alcohol and the local religion—commonly an amalgam of Catholicism and pagan rites. Illegitimate births, prostitution, robberies, and crimes of violence took an alarming increase during this period, while learned men disputed at length over the "inferiority" of these millions.[10] Infant mortality during the Díaz era hovered around fifty percent, and if we are to believe reports of that time, each living Indian must have been a walking catalog of parasites, diseases, and disorders.[11] This segment of the population represented the rotten timbers that would eventually bring down the entire structure erected by Díaz and his *científicos*. We shall later see, in part, how this took place.

II Heriberto Frías' Life: The Young Years

Heriberto Frías Alcocer was born in Querétaro on March 15, 1870. His family and relatives were of the respectable middle class in that area; most of them were lawyers, doctors, notaries, or governmental functionaries, and only his uncle, don Hilarión Frías y Soto (a noted historian, critic, and journalist), could at this time claim a degree of fame for the Frías family. Heriberto's mother was doña Dolores Alcocer and his father was don Antonio Frías, a former military commandant and supporter of the Lerdo de Tejada government. Heriberto spent the first fourteen years of his life in Querétaro. A timid and retiring youth, he was given to transports of romantic dreaming, and as a schoolboy he spent much of his time in the company of a small retinue of friends who, after the fashion of the times, wrote patriotic odes and love poetry.[12]

In 1884, the declining health of the father brought the Frías family to Mexico City, where Heriberto was soon enrolled in the National Preparatory School. His father was forced, in spite of his declining health, to take a humble position as a notary's clerk.

Later in that same year don Antonio died, and the family was left in poverty. Doña Dolores soon returned to Querétaro to live with a sister, taking her two daughters, Josefina and María, with her. His mother's departure left Heriberto in the capital to continue his studies and to make his way alone. The shy boy found work as a street vendor of magazines and newspapers, and in the evenings, his shoulders bleeding from the heavy leather bag in which he carried his wares, he studied with books borrowed from his employer's shelves; it is no surprise that during this period he contracted conjunctivitis from reading by gaslight, causing difficulties of vision that were to plague him for the remainder of his life and leave him blind before his death.

As a student at the National Preparatory School, he associated with a group of young students devoted to romantic poetry and revolutionary politics whose most violent manner of expression took the form of throwing rotten fruit at the nation's legislators (one of whom was their teacher at the school) in protest against the English debt. Of his revolutionary tendencies he wrote later, "I dreamed, like other Preparatory schoolboys, of attacking the barracks (at the National Military Academy of San Ildefonso), which looked out over the Preparatory School."[13] He could not have known as a boy that he would some day hang his sword in the same barracks.

Heriberto soon found it impossible to continue his studies, and he left the school. Nonetheless his habit of voracious reading continued, while the romantic fare he consumed populated his imagination with dreams of princesses and heroes, of glory and riches.

Much of his time was now spent with his magazine bag on the streets of Mexico City and among the worst influences; while he was still fourteen years old, he began to drink quantities of pulque. Once, after having often visited the home of a friend, he became the "lover" of the "lady" of the household. She soon tired of him, however, and Heriberto found himself again on the streets. Not long after, he stole five pesos from his employer and was given an eight month term in the Belén Prison, where he became acquainted with marijuana and gambling in the filth and degradation of that infamous institution. Being somewhat better educated than his associates there, he wrote letters and verses for the inmates and the jailors alike, winning their respect in spite of his youth. He was known, first scornfully and later with affection, as "The one-eyed urchin."[14]

When released, Frías became a tickettaker at a theater, and since his work was at nights, his days were left free for reading and studying. In view of his poverty and prison record, further formal study would have been impossible had it not been for a friend of his father who intervened in behalf of the shy, studious adolescent. Through the influence of his benefactor, Heriberto entered the military academy on December 28, 1887, at the age of seventeen years.

III Books and Bugles

Certainly Heriberto deserved further schooling, but it is doubtful that the prestigious military academy would ordinarily have accepted an ex-magazine vendor and convicted thief. His past was kept secret from his instructors and schoolmates, but what he could not hide was his lack of physical coordination, his poor eyesight, and his timidity. He was often the brunt of ridicule from the more sportive and aristocratic student body. So, alone and friendless, he devoted himself to his reading and studies; ironically, however, his grades at this institution were never better than mediocre, because even though he loved learning, his personal habits were chaotic and undisciplined.

His mother's remarriage at this time no doubt aggravated his retiring nature. As a sensitive and quiet youth, he was more than normally devoted to her and looked upon her remarriage, to a man whom he believed to be drunken and brutish, as a type of desertion.

An attack of altruism (and no doubt the desire for acceptance) once caused the youthful cadet to write an open letter to the academy officials, protesting a certain mass punishment being administered to his class. The unhappy result was that the officials singled him out to be further castigated, and far from winning the respect of his schoolmates, he reaped even more ridicule. Nevertheless, as a fruit of these experiences, his political and social ideas were beginning to take shape; he thought of himself as a "free thinker" and joined the disciples of Guillermo Prieto, his professor of history and a well-known Liberal. Frías' compassion for the poor and the downtrodden and his dislike for the well-to-do, views which were to figure in nearly all of his future writings, were sharpened as a result of his isolation and unhappiness as a cadet.[15]

After a year of military studies, he left the academy and joined the army, on January 16, 1889, as a sublieutenant in the Ninth Infantry Battalion. On his first night of barracks life he was brought to discipline for drunkenness, for though he still entertained dreams of military glory and heroism, he rebeled at the rigid behavior that was expected of him. Repeatedly punished on charges of drunkenness and poor military bearing, he was sentenced several times to the prison of Santiago Tlaltelolco. He also spent considerable time in the company of female friends and was consequently confined to a hospital to be treated for syphilis. For better or for worse, Frías seems to have seldom lacked for a woman's companionship, for José Valadés writes that "in his youth he was too attractive, particularly as a soldier, to resist the temptations offered to him by women."[16]

Frías' health was not robust, and it began at this time to suffer from his excesses; while in jail or in the hospital, his strength would return, only to be battered again on his release. On one occasion, he was given a truly extended convalescence in the form of a sentence in the Belén prison where, for the second time at that place, he witnessed "the crudest misery of our country's life, and learned of the worst infamies, and realized how people suffered through lack of health and instruction, and are exploited, squeezed, and condemned to injustice and death for their poverty."[17] Although he was sentenced for a period of one year and eighty days (the charge was "resisting arrest"), he contracted typhoid fever and was transferred to the Juárez Hospital.

When he finally returned to military duty, he encountered still another defeat; he met the daughter of a respectable family from Querétaro and began planning to make her his sweetheart. Unfortunately, his personal habits horrified the girl's parents, and the romance did not materialize.

IV *Campaign in the North*

While still a sublieutenant in Mexico City, Frías had begun to publish his short stories and poems in *El Combate*, a semiliterary periodical directed by General Sóstenes Rocha.[18] However on October 3, 1892, Frías' battalion left the capital and traveled north, first by train and then on foot, to join the other forces of the government engaged in a campaign in the state of Chihuahua against the rebellious inhabitants of Tomochic. During the battles and siege that followed, the little village was overwhelmed and destroyed by the federal troops. Here Frías saw for the first time the raw truth of military life, and his dreams of glorious battle crumbled in the reality of death and plunder. Forced by his duty as a soldier to commit barbarous acts, he became at once witness, participant, and victim in the brief but savage little war against Mexicans whom he respected and pitied.[19]

By November the campaign was completed, and Frías' battalion was withdrawn to the city of Chihuahua, capital of the state. There, on November 12, 1892, he received the rank of lieutenant. The death in battle of his friend and protector, a certain Captain Molina, plus the news that his mother had rejoined her new husband after a brief separation and was about to leave the country with him, again broke Frías' fragile spirit. Submerging his grief in alcohol, often pawning his dress uniform and sword, he disintegrated into a pitiful shadow of an officer, scorned even by the soldiers of the garrison. He became ill and was taken in by a compassionate camp follower, Concepción Montejo.[20] "Concha" encouraged him to reduce his drinking and slowly nursed him back to a semblance of health and military respectability.

One day Frías' read a newspaper article describing the recent campaign of Tomochic. Seeing that the facts of the event were distorted, he wrote a detailed account of his experiences to Joaquín Clausell, editor of a belligerent oppositionist newspaper in Mexico City, *El Demócrata*. Writing hurriedly during his nights on duty, he finished his thinly fictionalized chronicle in little more than a week and sent it to Clausell. Soon thereafter he received an enthusiastic reply from the editor, who to Frías' great surprise called the work a novel and informed the young author that *Él Demócrata* would publish his story in installments.

The installments, stated only that they were "written by an eyewitness," but not long after (April 16), General Rangel, who was the commanding officer of the Second Military Zone, rode into the garrison in the company of the local governor, Miguel Ahumada. Within minutes, Frías' was apprehended and deposited under guard in an empty cavalry stable. All indications were that he was to be shot, and during the following night his apartment was searched for letters or documents that might prove his guilt and send him without further ceremony to the firing squad, but no evidence was found, and the order to execute Frías was changed to a court martial. The Office of *El Demócrata* in Mexico City was ordered closed, and its editor, Clausell, was imprisoned pending a search of the office and an interrogation of the newspaper's staff, but these efforts produced no evidence either.[21]

Frías' novel as published in this bellicose newspaper contained information that was extremely embarrassing to General Rangel, Governor Ahumada, and the Díaz regime in general. While the series of campaigns against several insurgent villages in Chihuahua was being kept under a veil of semisecrecy by the government, *El*

Demócrata had repeatedly issued sharp protests, crowning its efforts with the publication of *Tomochic*. Furthermore, the last issues of the paper promised similar accounts of campaigns occurring elsewhere in the North. There is little wonder, then, that the arrests took place, but who ordered them and for what reason has not been clear until recently (see Chapter 2). As it was, after nine months of testimonies and trial, the officers of the court martial concluded that insufficient evidence was available and acquitted Frías' by a unanimous vote.[22]

Notwithstanding the favorable verdict, Frías was discharged from military service by the secretary of war. Finding himself nearly friendless in Chihuahua, he returned to his dipsomania. He obtained a minor position on the staff of *El Porvenir de Chihuahua*, where he was given the menial task of writing praises of local political bosses and other such dignitaries. Soon Governor Ahumada called Frías to his office and gave him money with which to leave the state, saying that he had best leave once and for all.[23] Frías bade a hurried farewell to his mistress Concepción and left for Mexico City.

V Life in Sodom—Mexico City—Tenochtitlán

At first, the atrocities laid bare in *Tomochic* had attracted a storm of public outrage in the capital, and with it, Frías had acquired great fame for himself. Unfortunately, his arrival in Mexico City was more than a year after the publication of his novel, and except among a few journalists and writers, he was now little remembered. But arrive Frías did, bringing with him the firm intention of joining what he imagined to be the brotherhood of journalists, champions of justice and proclaimers of truth.

It was in the office of *Gil Blas*, a Mexico City newspaper, that Frías began to see the error of his dreams. There, late in the year 1894, he was set to his first task as a big city newspaperman: that of cutting articles from other papers to be used in *Gil Blas* and of composing short items of interest concerning well-known personages, treating each individual favorably or unfavorably on orders from the editor. Such articles were printed unsigned, and it is just as well that Frías' efforts at this time should remain unidentifiable. The account that he leaves in *Miserias de México* (*Miseries of Mexico*) is enough to show his disappointment at being given such a routine position after expecting a triumphant welcome into the "brotherhood."[24] Frías anonymity was broken only when the newspaper moved its office to another location on March 19, 1895, and an article mentioned him as being on the staff and as having participated in the ensuing celebration.²⁵

During his stay with this newspaper, Frías also busied himself in the rewriting and expanding of his novel. This second edition of *Tomochic* was published in 1894.²⁶ During the same year he published two poems in the highly acclaimed literary periodical *El Siglo XIX*.

In 1895, Frías joined the newly reopened *El Democrata*, now headed by José Ferrel. Here he was welcomed as a sort of *enfant terrible*, for the members of this paper had good reason to remember *Tomochic*. Also, he fitted in well with the uproarious atmosphere of the office, for all concerned were oppositionists, polemicists, and confirmed Bohemians. On the desks were paper, rubbish, and empty bottles, and the air was laden with a heady mixture of the odors of smoke, ink, and alcohol. Frías gave himself over wholeheartedly to these delights to the point that he seldom knew what he had written until his articles appeared in print. Applauded as the child prodigy among the staff, he was led to believe that his most tasteless and pointless attacks were much better than they actually were. Inevitably, Frías' health proved to be vulnerable to the nightly sprees, and at one time editor Ferrel found it necessary to send Frías off to a prison cure for drunkenness.²⁷

A portrait of Frías printed in *El Demócrata* (December 15, 1895) shows him as a slender and handsome young man with sharply defined, almost delicate features. In life, as he describes himself during these years, he was often less presentable: ". . . a dirty shirt when he wore one, covered poorly by a long terry-cloth necktie, trousers so filthy they were stiff, rough shoes that were twisted and muddy."²⁸ Nevertheless, his star seemed to be rising, for during this year he published his second novel in the pages of *El Demócrata*: it was *Naufragio (Derelict)*, later to be rewritten and entitled *El amor de las sirenas (The Love of Sirens)*.²⁹

On May 8, 1895, an incident occurred that was to inspire one of Frías' better novels. As a result of a supposed insult, Colonel Francisco Romero and José Verástegui, two prominent citizens of the capital, fought a duel with pistols, and Verástegui was killed. A number of newspapers condemned the killing, and public indignation rose to the point where Romero was tried and convicted of homicide. Soon thereafter, President Díaz signed a law prohibiting all duels.³⁰

The duel affected Frías in two ways. The dramatic newspaper descriptions of the occurrence, especially in *El Monitor Republicano*, inspired him to compose a novel presenting a series of events drawing two protagonists inexorably into a tragic duel. This novel appeared in 1896 as *El último duelo (The Last Duel)*.[31] The other effect of the duel dealt with Frías' newspaper, for the event touched off a lengthy polemic between *El Demócrata* and *El Monitor Republicano* that ultimately sent the former's staff to jail on charges of libel and caused the fiery publication to close its doors once again.[32]

For the next three years Frías worked for the newspaper *El Combate* and produced a steady stream of articles and novels, including one short story and two poems published in the fashionable *El Mundo Ilustrado*. In 1897, he began turning out weekly articles concerning Indian legend and history with the titles "Leyenditas históricas" ("Little Historical Legends") and "Leyendas históricas" ("Historical Legends"), the latter appearing for nearly a year on the front page of every Sunday issue of *El Imparcial*. In 1899, a third edition of *Tomochic* was published and a number of his short stories appeared in *La Revista Moderna*.[33]

These were three years of great activity for Frías; for a time he had given up alcohol with its depressant effects and turned to the euphoria of morphine. For long periods he became a semirecluse and wrote furiously, hardly eating enough to stay alive. Under the sustained attack of morphine, Frías' mind and body surrendered slowly but inevitably, until he became desperately ill and entirely unable to care for himself. Once again a woman, this time Antonia Figueroa, coaxed him back to health. During the weeks of convalescence, Frías learned to appreciate and love his benefactress, and he finally asked her to marry him. But Antonia, a widow with unhappy memories of one dissolute husband, had no yearning for another such partner. Not until he had definitively given up his vices would she consent. Thus motivated, Frías placed himself in the care of a doctor and entered a sanitarium. Upon his release, he and Antonia were married in a civil ceremony.[34]

Frías' years of uneven habits and frequent escapades, plus his growing notoriety as a vitriolic critic of the regime, resulted in his not being able to find a position that would adequately support him and his bride. First as a lowly proofreader and then as a common reporter for *El Imparcial* (an "official" newspaper that Frías despised), he worked desperately to gain an honest livelihood in a business where not many were so scrupulous. Around him he saw that other reporters, a lean and hungry lot, supplemented their meager salaries by blackmail, threats of "exposure," and the creation of scandals. To his credit, Frías would have none of this, nor would he now join his colleagues on their nightly drinking sprees. For these reasons, he was not popular among his associates. Nor did his timidity allow him to be a successful reporter among his more aggressive competitors, and it was only through selling free lance articles when and where he could, plus churning out such diverse efforts as advertisements for the Orrín Circus and a large series of very hastily written "dime novel" booklets, *La biblioteca del niño mexicano* (*The Mexican Child's Library*),[35] that he succeeded in sustaining, however poorly, his wife and himself.

Commencing a search for a patron to sponsor his works and to finance their publication, Frías now wrote glowing praises to General Díaz and his minister of war, General Bernardo Reyes, in his prologue to *Episodios militares mexicanos* (*Mexican Military Episodes*)[36]; and in a short work dedicated to the dictator's deceased brother, *El general Félix Díaz* (*General Félix Díaz*),[37] Frías outdid himself in homage to the dictator. On another occasion, hoping to gain the favor of a rich northern Mexican, he composed a work concerning the military heroes of the North, but fled in panic at the first gruff word from his intended benefactor.

In November of 1902, Frías rejoined the military service and worked at the Secretariat of War and Navy until February of 1903, at which time he was given a medical discharge. His eyesight had deteriorated and he could now see only vague shapes.[38] An ensuing attempt was then made to gain a position in Justo Sierra's Secretariat of Public Instruction, which at that time was a refuge for unemployed artists and intellectuals. But Frías had often been critical of Sierra, so no job was forthcoming.

Antonia became ill, and the resulting medical expenses worsened the family's financial situation. Ultimately, a serious operation was performed, and Frías' financial desperation was complete. Casting about for a means to pay his debts, he hit upon Mexico City's current rage and scandal, the *género chico*, or vaudeville theater.[39] Once more dreaming of glory and riches, Frías quit his newspaper and set to work, in collaboration with a musical composer, at the task of writing a play entitled "Zarzuela" ("Interlude"). The play was never performed, very likely because it was a comic variation of the Adam and Eve story and bordered on heresy. The second attempt, "El Caimán" ("The Cayman"), was an underworld farce that was whistled and jeered out of existence on its first showing.

Soon after this defeat in the theater, Frías left the republic's capital for Mazatlán, where in 1906 he became editor of *El Correo de la Tarde*. The editorship of a newspaper gave him a long-awaited free rein on his polemic nature, and he became widely known as an oppositionist.

VI Change of Climate

Frías was delighted with Mazatlán, with its tropical coastline and its slow rhythm of life, and he later described many of the city's delights in *El triunfo de Sancho Panza (The Triumph of Sancho Panza)*. Above all, here he was able to enjoy a normal family life with his wife and children (Eva and Saúl), far from the Mexico City that had dealt him successive defeats and frustrations. Frías was a constant guest in the home of Andrés Valadés, a respected publisher, and owner of *El Correo de la Tarde*. Here Frías was the center of attention with his wit and "asphalted prose," as José Valadés (then a child) remembers it. The elder Valadés, recognizing Frías' talent, encouraged him to write and to channel his impetuous lifestyle and flighty habits into creative work. At times Frías closed himself into a room to write feverishly for days on end, while Valadés saw that food was brought to him. At his home on the Old Post Street (now Fifth of May Street), he also came to know Aurea Delgado, niece of his landlady. Aurea, a pretty and intelligent girl, worked as his secretary, and not long after she was to become his wife.[40]

A portrait of Frías that first appeared in *Tomochic's* fourth edition[41] shows the author at about thirty-five years. No longer the dapper lieutenant, he is plump, mustached, his spectacles betraying the myopia that increasingly harrassed him, and his sharp features of former years now lost in heavy jowls and a multiple chin. This pudgy exterior and his outwardly affable character, however, only superficially masked the nervous and volcanic soul that still roiled within.

No doubt Frías would have willingly stayed in peaceful Mazatlán for the rest of his life, but the drums of conflict were beating; the death of Francisco Cañedo, longtime governor of Sinaloa, left the position open in the elections of 1909, and Heriberto Frías became leader of an opposition campaign supporting his friend and ex-editor of *El Demócrata*, José Ferrel, despite the obvious danger of government reprisal. Their opponent was the dictator's chosen candidate, Diego Redo. During the campaign, Frías' oratory in favor of Ferrel was both vigorous and eloquent, and his heroic efforts in the face of government threats won for him the praise of another oppositionist, the candidate for president, Francisco I. Madero. However, Frías' bold efforts were in vain; the elections proved to be a sham, and he was unceremoniously driven from the state when Redo won.[42]

VII *Revolution and Victory*

Returning to Mexico City, Frías assumed for a time the editorship of *El Progreso Latino* as he continued his impassioned support of Francisco Madero. His well-publicized exploits in Mazatlán, together with new editions of his novels, strengthened his prestige; consequently, Frías took his place in the small cadre of leading oppositionists who nipped unceasingly at the despot's flanks. On October 29, 1910, *El Constitucional* published his mocking proposal to hold a contest among the Mexican states to determine "Which State Suffers the Most Ignominies?" With his characteristic broad irony, Frías envisioned a closely run competition: "Just imagine, for example, the rivalry between the bossdoms of Puebla and Yucatán. Neither wants to be less. Each wants to be worse. To one outrage in Puebla they will reply with a triple calamity in Mérida."[43]

As a leading figure among the regime's most troublesome detractors, he also became vice president of the Associated Press of Mexico, an organization made up of journalists with oppositionist leanings. In April of 1910, he was a leading member of a group representing the Associated Press that paid a personal visit to President Díaz on behalf of the numerous journalists then in jail. The group boldly asked that the newspapermen be freed in honor of the coming centennial celebrations of Mexico's independence. They were courteously received, but Díaz took no action. Frías then opened an active campaign of protest, bravely urging journalists throughout the republic to send telegrams to officials in favor of the prisoners' release. Again, no response from the dictatorship was forthcoming, and the matter was dropped. All the while, Frías stayed on as editor of *El Progreso Latino* and sent many articles to *El Espectador* and *El Constitucional*, which at the time was being directed by his friend Rafael Martínez, known by the pseudonym "Rip-Rip."

In the months preceding the grand centennial celebration, Frías' pen dripped acid. Knowing that Díaz intended to exploit the occasion with a welter of ceremonies, dedications, and parades, Frías' usual device was to seize upon some aspect of the coming festivities and to make it an object of ridicule. The Palace of Fine Arts, for example, was to be dedicated during the peak of the celebrations, but it had already begun to sink into the marshy valley's subsoil. Frías saw the gaudy, domed building as a "golden helmet, too big and too heavy, that a triumphant party is trying to wear in order to frighten the downtrodden and impress foreigners." The palace's settling was, to Frías, symbolic of Mexico itself:

That splendid larva, which has devoured so many millions and threatens to gobble up so many more, is growing old woefully and precociously, even before its useless, ultramodern and Babylonic gaudiness supplants the old heroic spirit of the national eagle. . . . Because, there is no doubt that those sacred halls are not for Paco Gavilanes [a well-known comic actor] to let forth his salty jokes and escapades, or for any young Ursula to show her thighs at seventy-five cents per balcony seat.[44]

The year 1910 was a feverish one for Frías, and it was not without tragedy. On about June 10, Antonia, whose health had been poor for some time, died at their home in Tacuba. Rafael Martínez wrote in *El Constitucional's* issue of June 12, 1910, that she had been a faithful companion throughout Frías' hard years of persecution.[45]

On August 4, after a pause following his wife's death, Frías renewed his attacks on the regime. He first singled out Justo Sierra:

It has been officially declared that there are no Mexican poets capable of producing stanzas of an anthem to the national independence that would be worthy of being sung during the centennial celebration. But the fact is that there are more than enough "poets." One need only go to the offices of the Ministry of Education to be convinced that from His Pontifical Highness [Sierra] down to the lowest Rubén M. Campos [a poet whom Frías disliked], they are all bards. Yes, there are plenty of them, but what they lack is adherence to the truth, patriotic souls, manly stirrings; and that is what cannot be found among the gardens of the court, nor among its poets.[46]

A few days later he added, speaking of the University of Mexico's reopening: "Don Justo only thinks of the university and of fabricating doctors at his pleasure. . . . These degrees have so proliferated that even before its birth that university has lost its prestige, and it will be a title of honor not to belong to it."[47]

In September, Rafael Martínez, editor of *El Constitucional*, exhausted the patience of the dictatorship and was jailed. Frías took his position on September 23 and continued to condemn the hollowness of the centennial in almost daily editorials. He assailed every aspect of its fanfare and glitter, from its speeches to its commemorative *peso* (which, significantly, had been designed by a foreigner): "to some malignant, mocking spirit the reverse side [of the coin] might look, from a distance, like a tailless turkey eating an earthworm." He also offered an interpretation of the coin's other side as symbolic of Mexico's lamentable state of affairs, for it contained "a sinking sun, a walking horse, a genie who has released the bridle to carry a torch . . . and in the background, a face looking toward the past." "The thought," he observed wryly, "is profound and terrible."[48]

Once the speeches and parades were over, Frías, repulsed and indignant, put his finger directly into the wounds of his country and spelled out the suffering that Díaz had tried to hide from visiting dignitaries, and openly assailed as hypocritical the boom and blare of the great showcase celebrations that Díaz hoped would impress the world:

> Everything in the recent centennial festivals was official, artificial, diplomatic, and vacuous; everything resounded like something empty, like dying, bloated bellies, and the gaiety itself wore a grimace of forced laughter, false and contrived.
>
> Within that posturing, swelled by financial strainings and diplomatic gravity, remained the penury of the middle classes for whom there is only hunger, and the sorrow and shame of the people's civic consciousness, contemplating in the glare of gigantic lights and to the sound of bugles and drums . . . the cadaver of public liberty.[49]

On October 4, the chamber of deputies announced the reelection of Porfirio Díaz as president and the *científico* Ramón Corral as vice president; this announcement caused Frías to assail the *científicos*, whom he despised. Having often attacked them before, he now beleagured them almost daily, calling them "Neotraitors," "The Fatal Bond," and worse (with a reference to their dedication to commerce), "Judas, Barrabas, and Company." Seeing their rise to power as a catastrophe overshadowing even that of Díaz himself, now that the "perpetual president" was advanced in age, and fearful that the *científicos* would shortly introduce their own particularly malignant brand of Positivist tyranny, Frías wrote:

> Now, as never before in recent years, an intense uneasiness is felt in the country, in the center as well as the periphery. . . . Even ten years ago the governors and their political chiefs were Porfirists to the core; they governed militarily, but there was a certain discipline and even a certain love for the Supreme Chief. . . . Many loved him, all feared him, only the *científicos* or NEOTRAITORS hated him, behind their masks.
>
> Today, now that they [the *científicos*] have triumphed, now that all the governors and deputies are "scientists," now that the [dictator's] will does not come down straight and direct, but rather broken and twisted by the veto of the clique that drains his power, the dictatorship is shadier because it is hypocritical.[50]

In the face of an apparent Positivist takeover, Frías surprisingly turned to Díaz' defense. When the irascible Francisco Bulnes began to denounce the dictator, Frías retaliated:

> . . . now that the dictator has grown old and blind as a King Lear and is betrayed by his own court, now it turns on him. . . . But now, since it is necessary for the "scientists" to prepare for a successor,—Pineda or Corral?—as they watch over the dying king, they find it advantageous to begin stripping away his prestige and to call him Tyrant. . . . Thus the origin of Bulnes' latest book, the Bulnes who in the last moments of Porfirism declares himself an Anti-Porfirist. The leap is dizzying, paradoxical. The court prepares for the monarch's funeral by denouncing him, even while it whispers into his ear, trying to make him tremble, "revolution!"[51]

These were busy days. Frías' newspaper, *El Constitucional*, advertising itself as the "official" paper of the antireelectionist party, reproduced Madero's speeches and declarations, sold his book *La sucesión presidencial en 1910*, and even offered a bust in his likeness. At the same time Frías looked out for his own interest; the paper advertised his novels, which were for sale in the office, and in the paper itself were reproduced parts of *Los piratas del boulevard* (*The Pirates of the Boulevard*, not to be published until 1915),[52] *Episodios militares mexicanos*, and *El amor de las sirenas*. His powers of descriptive caricature and heavy-fisted satire made him one of the more popular journalists of the city; his Quevedolike social satires, such as those later collected in *Los piratas del boulevard*, were written to be read allegorically, and when they produced the desired effect, he wrote, "those initiated, the office staff and even the court of those involved know the key, decipher voluptuously . . . and everyone, even the victims, applaud the able chronicler."[53]

To add to the activity, Frías kept up a running verbal battle with the "official" newspapers of the city. From Reyes Spíndola of *El Imparcial* he received private insults, and from *El Debate*, public ones, calling him *"El teniente Mochila"* ("Lieutenant Knapsack") and calling public attention to Frías' scarlet past.[54] During these months, he also produced the fifth edition of *Tomochic*[55] and another novel, *El triunfo de Sancho Panza (The Triumph of Sancho Panza)*.

Somehow during these months Frías found time for more personal pursuits, for on, October 30, 1910, he married Aurea Delgado in a civil ceremony at Tacuba. The church wedding took place on the following Thursday in the presence of María de Rodríguez and Dr. Secundino Rodríguez, Frías' sister and brother-in-law.[56]

The days that followed, however, hardly constituted a honeymoon for either Frías or for Mexico. Vice President Corral, now clearly pulling the reins of the tottering government, began to strike back at the oppositionists, who in past months had become increasingly impertinent. Francisco Madero, who had been in hiding since an aborted demonstration on September 11, made good his escape to the United States early in October. From exile he proclaimed his *Plan de San Luis Potosí*, calling for nullification of the June elections and for the overthrowing of the Díaz-Corral government. Several newspapers, including *El Diario del Hogar* and *El Mexicano*, were closed down, and *El Constitucional* ceased operations from October 31 (the day following Frías' marriage) to November 9. Actually, Frías' widow recounts that she, a twenty-two year old bride, and her forty year old husband had (under orders from Madero) taken the train north just hours after their wedding. In order to escape through the city and to pass by governmental pursuers, he disguised himself in the uniform and cape of a police officer, and Aurea covered her identity with a peasant's dress and heavy wool shawl.[57] From his hiding place in the North, Frías then wrote: "Difficulties inherent to the free press forced us to suspend publication of our paper for a few days. . . . The jail, in a way, presents a sinister threat to us; nevertheless, we stand before the situation, waiting the triumph of our ideals."[58]

In the same day's issue, he spoke out against the approaching threat of revolution in an article obviously referring to Madero's call to arms: "No one can deny that democratic sentiment exists among the people, nor that citizens are able to exercise the right to vote from their own convictions and evidencing great responsibility. . . . But we recognize one danger, the danger of impatience to which restless spirits are so prone, but we deny the right to violence as a means of salvation. Patriotism counsels us to persist in the true democratic attitude that respects peace and order as bases of prosperity."[59]

By this time, however, it was too late to ask for Olympian serenity; arrests continued in the capital, and rumors circulated of uprisings in Chihuahua. On the following day, *El Constitucional* announced simply that Jesús Rodríguez Tinoco was now its editor and that Frías, "whose private affairs now take him away from this journalistic task" was no longer on the staff.[60] Frías' flight took him north to the state of Coahuila where a number of antireelectionists were seeking refuge from governmental persecution. There he awaited further orders from Madero.

The Maderist revolt triumphed, and Frías returned to ride the political crest. He was appointed undersecretary of foreign affairs and became a member of President Madero's Central Committee. Soon thereafter he was named as government fiscal agent in Mazatlán (after having been offered governorship of Sinaloa, which he refused). Arriving in Mazatlán, he was given a riotous hero's welcome.[61]

President Madero, for his part, proved to be a lukewarm reformer and an inept leader. Unwittingly, this reluctant revolutionary committed a series of blunders that paved the way for General Victoriano Huerta's treacherous counterrevolt on February 11, 1913, when the latter usurped the presidency. Huerta wasted no time in murdering Madero and, supported by conservative elements, returning the country to a military dictatorship fashioned after that of Porfirio Díaz. Only now did the true issues of the revolution begin to take shape, as the financial, commercial, military, and clerical powers rallied behind Huerta, whereas support for the anti-Huerta forces came from the mines, factories, and especially the agricultural communities, among whose leaders were Venustiano Carranza, Francisco Villa, Emiliano Zapata, and Alvaro Obregón. In many parts of the republic rebellions broke out, challenging Huerta's new dictatorship.

As Madero's government crumbled, Frías discovered that he and other Maderists were marked for persecution, and so he escaped by boat to San Francisco, from where he reentered Mexico and made his way to Sonora, a stronghold of anti-Huerta "constitutionalists." There, Frías assumed the editorship of Hermosillo's *La Voz de Sonora* and came to know "The First Chief" (Venustiano Carranza, as this revolutionary leader insisted he be called) when the latter arrived to organize his revolutionary government in September of 1913.[62]

VIII *Aguascalientes and Defeat*

When the various revolutionary factions gathered at Aguascalientes in October 1914, Frías became editor of its official newspaper, *La Convención,* which proclaimed and analyzed the proceedings of each day's meeting. When Venustiano Carranza split with Villa and Zapata, and was subsequently pursued to coastal Veracruz, Frías became a partisan of the tenuous North-South alliance of Villa and Zapata, bitterly criticising Carranza as both a reactionary and a traitor: "The elderly and nominal chief of a triumphant insurrection, drunk with joy and power, surrounded by a court *a lo* Huerta, blinded by self-dazzlement, persisted in being the Only Leader, ignored the assembly of popular and faithful leaders, and rebeled against it. He fought against it with his mercenaries' swords and pens, and what is worse, with the same treasures ripped from the entrails of his people."[63]

From Aguascalientes to San Luis Potosí, and from there to Querétaro, Mexico City, and Cuernavaca, the Sovereign Convention moved its assembly about, doing so first for political reasons but soon fleeing from Carranza's growing forces. Frías, his staff, and *La Convención's* bulky printing press accompanied each move. Frías followed through his editorials, the vicissitudes of that stormy body of deliberators. As editor of the official newspaper, Frías voiced enthusiastic approval of each of the convention's resolutions, while constantly exhorting the members to end the petty animosities that time and again threatened to bring the sessions to an abrupt end. Frías often attempted to mollify the volatile Zapatists and Villists by flattery and praise: "The men of this revolution, and most especially the men of the convention, must have a mountaineer's frankness, *Plan de Ayala* style; a northerner's sincerity, Villa style, lacking in ceremony, freed from ritual, that is, able to believe and to say, by word and deed, that while the constitution is being reborn the convention deliberates, governs, and commands."[64]

On January 25, 1915, Frías assumed the editorship of *El Monitor*, another conventionist newspaper, continuing for several months as the head of both *El Monitor* and *La Convención*. In these months, too, *Los piratas del boulevard*, a collection of his satirical newspaper sketches, made its appearance in book form.

Unfortunately, by mid-1915 the "Sovereign Convention" was far into its eclipse. Carranza's troops occupied Mexico City and at the same time were crushing Villa in the North. In the spring months of that year, Frías' editorials appeared only infrequently, though not diminished in their enthusiasm, and on May 18, 1915, he was replaced by Rafael Pérez Taylor as editor of *El Monitor*, while the convention and its declining membership took refuge in Toluca and ultimately dispersed.[65]

Very likely much of Frías' time and energy were now being devoted to a new novel, for the following advertisements appeared in *La Convención* of June 5, 1915, and in subsequent issues:

THE DELUGE IN MEXICO

(History and Criticism of Things and Men of the Revolution and the Convention of 1913–1915)

By Heriberto Frías

The purpose of this work is to publicize facts and commentaries about the revolution and the convention as written by a firsthand witness. The form adapted is novelesque so as to circulate it among the middle and lower classes, the worker class, and the citizens of the revolutionary army.

This is the continuation of the series initiated by its author with "Tomochic" in 1892, "The Love of Sirens," written in 1906 in Sinaloa, and "The Triumph of Sancho Panza," published in Mazatlán in 1908.

The first part of "The Deluge in Mexico" will be divided into the following books:

I In the North
II Sodom-Tenochtitlán

III Aguascalientes and San Luis Potosí
IV The Specter of Ahuizotl and
V Cuernavaca

Book One, containing many illustrations and historical documents, will appear soon.

"Ahuizotl" (the name of a particularly bloodthirsty Aztec king) was an epithet that Frías often used in his newspaper articles to denote Carranza, so the fourth book of "El diluvio en México" apparently recalled Carranza's struggle with the convention. We can thus be assured that the projected novel was highly uncomplimentary to the "First Chief." Not surprisingly, the book never appeared, and the manuscript was lost. The reason for this was that Carranza triumphed over the convention and became president, bringing Frías' repeated attacks home to roost. The luckless author again took flight; Frías fled for weeks with remnants of Villa's army through the mountains north of Mexico City. One cold night he, ill and blind, and Aurea became separated from the others, and wandered aimlessly, leading their horses along narrow and slippery mountain trails. Finally Aurea saw the lights of a house and they approached. At this hacienda, near Ixmiquilpa, Frías surrendered, was freed (under a general amnesty then in effect), and was almost immediately recaptured, as Carranza's hate caught up with him. On the day following his apprehension, armed military guards paraded him ceremoniously through Mexico City's main streets and deposited him in the capital's penitentiary. A military trial ensued, with Frías accused of "rebellion." Finally the court, reminded by numerous influential witnesses of Frías' merits as an author, handed down a verdict of acquittal. Nonetheless, an order from "general headquarters" (i.e., Carranza) returned him to prison with a twelve year sentence, a dear price for his scathing articles against the "First Chief."

Since Frías' poor vision and weakened physical state made him all but unable to care for himself, his wife was permitted to stay with him in the cell during the long months that followed. Fortunately, influential friends again interceded on his behalf and protested the arbitrary sentence, with the result that after eight months, Frías was freed.[66]

On his release Frías retired from politics and journalism, withdrawing to Azcapozalco to dictate more writings to Aurea and to raise chickens. Seeking solace from his troubled memories, Frías listened each evening as his wife read poems by the poet Amado Nervo. Though not a religious man—in his youth he had professed a rebellious form of atheism—Frías found great comfort in Nervo's tendencies to mystic pantheism. In 1918 he published *La vida de Juan Soldado (The Life of Juan the Soldier)*, a short booklet based on a popular legend.[67] During this time he also began to write his planned trilogy on the Mexican Revolution, which because of his poor eyesight he had to dictate to his wife.

IX   The Later Years

The year 1920 saw the assassination of Carranza and the presidency of Alvaro Obregón. It also brought a change to Frías' fortunes, for Obregón sent him to Cádiz as Mexican consul, where he served until 1923. Now totally blind, Frías' greatest impression of Spain was that "everything smelled of olive oil." Despite his handicap, he and Aurea traveled to Madrid, Barcelona, and Paris, as Aurea dutifully described the sights to "the mollusk," as Frías came to call himself.[68] During his stay in Spain he finished *¿Aguila o sol? (Heads or Tails?)*, the first installment of a projected trilogy dealing with the Mexican Revolution. When this novel was printed, its back cover promised two more parts, entitled "El diluvio mexicano" ("The Mexican Deluge") and "La noche y el alba" (The Night and the Dawn"). Frías was seemingly resuscitating, in part or in whole, the novel that had been suppressed and lost eight years before.

Once again his health declined, and Frías returned from Spain to Tizapán, at that time a quiet country town on the outskirts of Mexico City. Still in need of financial support, he obtained a position with the Public Relations Department of Mexico City where he worked in collaboration with Rafael Martínez, his friend of stormy Maderist days. Also, in spite of his blindness, he worked as editor of *La Revista del Ejército y de la Marina (The Army-Navy Review)*. In the spring of 1925, he and Martínez produced their *Album histórico popular de la Ciudad de México (Popular Historical Album of Mexico City)*, a commemorative work sponsored by the city government to celebrate the six hundredth anniversary of the city's founding.[69]

The *Album* was Frías' last published work; a scant five months after its appearance, he lay dead in his home at Reforma 20, Tizapán, a victim of entercolitis. His death occurred at 10:30 on the morning of November 12, 1925, at the age of fifty-five. Frías' death was noted with "consternation" among friends and fellow journalists, said *El Universal* of the following day in a short notice relating some highlights of his life. The Frías home was the scene of the wake. The walls of the dwelling were covered with black cloth, and the coffin was placed on columns among candles and wreaths. Among those paying their respects were a number of journalists and writers and a group of representatives from the Association of the Military Academy, to which Frías had belonged. Then, at two o'clock on the afternoon of November 14, Frías was taken in a cortege of streetcars to the French Pantheon, where he was buried.[70]

The deceased author left a touching tribute to his wife in *¿Aguila o sol?*, through which we can perceive the tenderness he felt for her. In the closing pages of the novel, Miguel Mercado (i.e., Frías) is told to go to Mazatlán (where Frías met Aurea), where he will find his future wife "Aurora." She is described to him in this manner: "She is a sensitive woman, all heart, all capacity to love and to pity, to suffer and console. . . . There she is dreaming of a worthy man, persecuted and unfortunate, someone to comfort, a blindman to guide."[71] It is happily apparent that Frías, to whom women had meant both ruin and salvation, had at last found the tranquility and love that had so long eluded him.

And so passed Frías from his disorderly existence. Like his writings, he was at once simple and complex. Timid, flighty, and almost passive in his personal dealings, he was bold, foolhardy, and warlike in defense of his beliefs and ideologies. It is as though he were at once vested with the souls of Sancho Panza and Don Quixote, so that his writings, as we shall see, is uneven but quite worthy of honor and appreciation.

CHAPTER 2

Tomochic

A young artillery officer of twenty-two years, Heriberto Frías participated in the dictatorship's campaign against the tiny village of Tomochic, which was merely one of several government attempts to stamp out pockets of resistance in the mountainous northlands. But for Frías, witnessing the clumsy and merciless destruction of this remote community was such a shock that he scrawled off a hurried account of the tragedy and with this, shook the nation. Half diary, half chronicle, *Tomochic*[1] was, in its first form, more of a personal confessional to rid its author of vivid, shattering memories than an attempt to create art. This is the story that readers of the newspaper *El Demócrata* found serialized in its pages.

As the account begins, the proud Ninth Batallion is on its way to Tomochic, and with it goes Miguel Mercado, a green and idealistic young lieutenant. The troops stay for a time in nearby Guerrero, where Miguel meets Julia and Bernardo Carranza. Miguel, unaware that they are partisans of the Tomochic rebels who have been sent to Guerrero to spy on the troop movement, falls in love with Julia.

The batallion again takes to the road and with some difficulty and confusion, reaches its target. A combined assault involving this force and other government troops fails because of poor leadership and ill-trained soldiers. In the midst of battle, Frías' dreams of military glory and heroism vanish as around him he sees mostly horror, confusion, and cowardice. Unable to defeat the *Tomochitecos* in open warfare, the federal troops resolve to encircle the hamlet, leaving the rest to starvation and artillery bombardment. In the following siege, Tomochic is systematically reduced to ruins, while Miguel secretly despairs for Julia, since he now knows that she is among the defenders. At one point, the surviving women and children of the town are allowed to surrender and file out under strict guard. Miguel gets only a glimpse of the starving horde, but he does not see Julia. The men of Tomochic, refusing to submit, continue to hold out until they are reduced to a handful. When finally captured, the last defenders, including their fanatic leader Cruz Chávez, are summarily shot. Tomochic exists only as burning rubble and rotting bodies.

Amidst looting, drunken celebrating, and the burning of piles of cadavers, Miguel searches for his sweetheart. Summoned to attend a dying woman among the surviving captives, Mercado finds that she is no other than Julia, wounded and delirious. She dies in Miguel's arms, and the story ends.

I Tomochic—*A Call to Revolt?*

Tomochic is a simple, poignant story of a young man at war, not unlike Stephen Crane's *Red Badge of Courage*. What, then, brought the political bosses to their feet in anger? Was Frías in some way the oracle of revolution? Critics' answers have been heated and often misguided. It has often been assumed that since Frías was persecuted because of the novel's publication, he himself was a quixotic rebel and prophet of the coming revolution. Mariano Azuela is at the fore of those who would canonize Frías, stating that in the novel one strongly feels the "prelude of a revolution," while René Avilés declares that *Tomochic* "pointed out with absolute precision the forces that were undermining the great Porfirian edifice." In sharp contrast, an anonymous critic wrote in 1919 that "the author of *Tomochic* does not expose the causes of the tragic war" and that he is "divorced from any intention to harm the government or the army." E. R. Moore, taking the same stance, maintains that "nowhere does Miguel Mercado, that is, Heriberto Frías, question the justice of the Federal Campaign."[2]

These conflicting attitudes are greatly due to the various critics' having read different editions of *Tomochic* (though, as we shall see, Moore's statement is vulnerable from any standpoint). Avilés admits he is referring only to the "definitive edition," while Azuela claims he is writing of the first edition, but his textual references correspond only to 1906 or 1911 versions. Thus Avilés and Azuela are clearly assuming that Frías was persecuted in 1893 for things he did not actually write into his novel until more than a decade later! None appear to have actually read the serialized *El Demócrata* story. The fact is that *Tomochic*'s criticism of the Díaz regime rose in pitch and volume through the 1899 version to a *fortissimo* of accusations and insinuations in the novel's final form, but since Frías was very nearly shot for what he said in the comparatively pallid 1893 edition, and since that edition created a national scandal, the exact nature of its criticism will here be noted in some detail.

In the first edition, by far the greatest attack is aimed at the army—the glorious bastion of the dictatorship—which, even while outnumbering the rebels by better than twenty to one, had extreme difficulty in winning its battles.[3] Frías shows graphically that the field commanders, and particularly the acting commander of the expedition, General José María Rangel, are utterly inept and clearly to blame for the repeated blunders that plagued the campaign. He shows how the initial assault became a bloody rout because Rangel's own troops arrived late for what should have been a synchronized attack, and this for the embarrassing reason that they had become lost on the mountain trails: "The advance guard descended the side of the mountain and penetrated the thickets of a small grove at its base. Then it was up another hill, when suddenly the column halted. What was going on? Did they see the enemy? No. We were on the wrong road and we had to countermarch, take the old way again and then veer to the right."[4]

Little wonder, for these were parade ground officers who had been stationed in Mexico City for eight years finding themselves suddenly out of place in the wilds of the North: "They were something to see, those officers, in the palace halls and on the sidewalks of the *Plateros* district, their waistcoats always buttoned, all slicked up and severe looking, showing off their gold emblems, their swords hanging from the belt; they were something to see on the arid, hard trail, dusty and dirty, disheveled, blackened by the sun. . . ."[5]

These same commanders, ridiculous on the march, became tragic in battle; instead of engaging the adversary in "classic" combat, they found themselves fighting on a steep slope in a dense woods. Lacking leadership, the poorly trained federals were soon firing on one another. Discipline, such as it was, disintegrated, and whole units deserted: "This was deathly chaos, a time of immense desperation! Not one voice of command to be heard, no one to be understood. . . ."[6]

Already in the first edition Frías questions the justice of the federal campaign and demonstrates open sympathy for the rebels' independent, albeit fanatic, actions. Indeed, he throws the blame upon others as he retells how one government official had violated a daughter of Cruz Chávez, how another had stolen paintings from their church, and how church and official provocation, coupled with the inhabitants' proud and warlike nature, gave rise to the tragedy, with "immense responsibility for those guilty!"[7] Here he accused no one openly (as he did in later editions), but clearly went counter to the "official" newspaper reportings of the event, which painted the northern rebels as savages and wanton criminals. Likewise, one might imagine the wrath of General Rangel and his staff as they saw their blunders paraded before the reading public of *El Demócrata!*

By criticizing in such a manner the representatives of the regime, Frías was surely aiming obliquely at the dictator himself. Thus a behind the scenes drama ensued that rivals that of the novel itself—a drama only recently made available to scholars through the opening of the Díaz Archives.[8]

II Díaz Strikes Back

Tomochic's serialized episodes ended on April 14, 1893. On the following day, Porfirio Díaz sent a furiously worded, top secret, and coded telegram from the palace in Mexico City to Governor Ahumada of Chihuahua, instructing him to "get together with Rangel and proceed energetically and decisively in the following way":

If Frías saw action in Guerrero . . . bring charges against Frías for cowardice regardless of his conduct in battle, and if Frías did not see action and he is still in that city, tell Rangel to search through his papers scrupulously and you help to search them; [I am] sure that you will find correspondence of Clausell [*El Demócrata*'s editor] and many of the drafts of the articles that he has been sending and possibly [others] about mutiny or [enough] for a trial.[9]

The telegram further makes clear that Díaz had already looked into the matter and had done some investigating of his own. He already knew who Frías was, that Frías had written something in the guardhouse office, and even who had loaned him the keys to work there. His extreme sensitivity, however, did not permit him to view *Tomochic* other than as journalistic "articles," and he demanded total secrecy and dispatch in dealing with Frías. As Frías was immediately jailed and was held incommunicado as searches took place both of Frías' quarters and of *El Demócrata*'s office in Mexico City, Díaz oversaw every move by coded telegrams and received detailed reports from Ahumada and Rangel.[10]

No trumped-up charge of cowardice such as Díaz ordered was attempted, but Frías was arraigned under articles 873, 968, 974, and 1056 of the Code of Military Justice, that is, "for rumors and criticism of his superiors; for having spread information of the sort that causes negligence in the service; for failing his military duties by revealing campaign secrets, and by intentionally and maliciously spreading false alarm."[11] As a soldier, Frías was vulnerable. *Tomochic* clearly constituted gross insubordination. A civilian might conceivably come away with lesser punishment, but for Frías, a soldier in a recognized combat zone, the penalty was death.

Frías pleaded innocent, and searches turned up no damning evidence, thanks to Frías' mistress Concha, who hid a letter from Clausell thanking the author for his manuscript in a basket of her soiled clothes, so that when the searchers started to rummage among the unmentionables, she feigned a woman's wounded dignity with such spirit that they stopped. No proof having been found, both Rangel and Ahumada advised that *El Demócrata*'s office be searched, Rangel twice reminding the dictator that if proper evidence were not produced, the supreme court would be likely to overthrow the military court's decision, since all they had to date were suppositions.[12]

Díaz' reply to this is a curious one. To Ahumada's reminder that the case would be stronger if the original draft were found, Díaz responded that "For originals you [Ahumada] must ask permission from someone who will hand them over to me. *I have an exact copy* but I cannot use it [as evidence] without permission. If they give it to me the proof will be complete."[13] Where or how Díaz obtained a copy of the manuscript is not said. But one fact stands clear: the dictator knew as much or more about Frías' complicity than either Ahumada or Rangel. He had used his own sources to put them onto Frías' track and to keep them there, but his control over the supreme court was not so complete as to permit a drumhead execution.

Surely Díaz had hoped that Frías could have been imprisoned, sentenced, and shot outright, but now the unpleasant matter had bogged down in legalities. But on the chance that proof lay in the office of *El Demócrata*, Díaz himself (at the behest of Rangel and Ahumada) ordered the paper closed and Clausell held for questioning. What he did not know was that the proof of Frías' guilt indeed lay in *El Demócrata*'s office; there, locked in a desk, were the manuscripts of *Tomochic*, written in Frías' handwriting—and what is more, on Ninth Batallion stationery. It was another journalist friend, Adalberto Concha, who broke into the locked office and pried open the desk to destroy the papers that would have sent Frías to the firing squad.

The greater part of Frías' lengthy court martial curiously was not aimed at proving that he had written *Tomochic*, but rather that he had provided Clausell with the "articles" with which the latter had written the novel. Since Frías was a soldier in a combat zone (Chihuahua), his divulgence of information was clear grounds for execution, and for that reason Clausell nobly declared himself to be the author, insisting that he had gleaned data from various sources, including newspapers published in the United States. He further declared that he and Frías had only exchanged letters concerning Frías' subscription to *El Demócrata*. Throughout the proceedings, Frías steadfastly denied all knowledge of the novel except for having read it as a subscriber.

Díaz followed the trial closely at first, since he ordered that complete reports be sent to him. But the threatening tone of his first telegram soon cooled to brief, almost nonchalant replies, and as soon as *El Demócrata*'s office was closed and its press was stilled, presidential interest in the affair apparently came to an end. At any rate, Porfirio Díaz had won a partial victory, since under pretext of having divulged military information, *El Demócrata* and its editor were silenced for a time. This was no trifling matter, as the newspaper had provided Clausell and his partner Querido Moheno with a ready outlet for strident attacks against the government, accusing various officials of graft and mismanagement. They had even taken on the dictator himself in recent articles and had with termerity spoken of possible widespread revolution: "*Tuxtépec* [i.e., Díaz] does not aspire, nor has he ever aspired to maintaining peace, nor is his prestige solid, founded on acts, but rather artificial and based on the squandering of national resources. What *Tuxtépec* has aspired to is to prolong the benefits of his chieftains, and with similar ignoble purposes, far from consolidating peace, he is sowing the seeds of revolution."[14]

Repeatedly defying attempted governmental cover-ups of its

northern campaigns, *El Demócrata* boldly published news of troop movements and reports of atrocities. Finally, its editors printed the anonymous *Tomochic* and then whetted its readers' appetite for more of the same fare by promising an account of a similar assault on the village of Temosachic. It was at this point, as we have seen, that the newspaper's office was ordered closed and its staff held "for questioning." Díaz' real anger was apparently with *El Demócrata*, and so ultimately the dictator got what he wanted in the suppression of that periodical.

Nonetheless, to say that Díaz saw *Tomochic* as a handy lever to squelch *El Demócrata* is in no way to diminish Frías' recklessness in directing public censure of the dignitaries of Chihuahua and in broadcasting the blunders of his superior officers. In doing so, he took Díaz' very nuclei of control—local bosses and the military—sternly to task. Does this support allegations that Frías envisioned or supported general revolution? This view has been inferred by David López Peimbert, who maintains that "his [Frías'] attitude is the disinterested one of the authentic revolutionary who only seeks the downfall of social order without regard to what the consequences might be that his attitude could provoke."[15] Such an interpretation may be inferred from later editions in which the possibility (but likewise futility) of mass insurrection is pondered, but the 1893 princeps beats no drum of revolution, particularly among the peasant masses, whom Frías was quite obviously content to admire from a distance.

What one *does* perceive goes far deeper than mere political skulduggery. It is a sense of uneasiness, a free-floating moral anxiety that unites all of Frías' earlier works. Frías is telling us—telling himself, really—that something is wrong in the very marrow of Mexican life. Soldiers who cannot fight and leaders who do not lead are only part of his concern. His is a world of deception, incompetency, apathy, ignorance, and vice, seeking not so much a change in political order as a return to basic virtue: bravery, common sense, loyalty, sacrifice. But when he finds it, he is overwhelmed. His characters who possess some virtue (Captain Molina, Julia, even Cruz) shine briefly and die, as though they cannot live in the moral pollution that engulfs them, or as if the author cannot adequately deal with them in the society he is striving to comprehend. Mercado, Frías' literary surrogate, seeks out these virtues in *Tomochic*, and in later novels, only to lose them again and again. Far from the revolutionary drive, Frías/Mercado's urge is that of the latent hero who casts about, not for an enemy to bring down, but for something worth fighting for. His criticisms, even at their most acerbic heights, spell disillusionment, not destruction.

III Tomochic *Evolves*

Untrammeled by the need for extreme caution as the dictator grew older and loosened his grip on public opinion, Frías repeatedly rewrote *Tomochic* and added numerous passages of criticism in other editions, zeroing in steadily upon the despot himself. After describing the hardships of the federal soldiers, he adds this caustic comment: "What blame did those souls have, who suffered and fought for such vague things, so high-flown, so incomprehensible for them, as the tranquility of the country, Order, Homeland, Progress, Duty?"[16]

The reference here clearly mocks Díaz' oft-repeated and well-publicized motto of "Liberty, Order, and Progress." At another point where a conversation among soldiers is added, someone remarks that Díaz himself might well be directing the campaign by telegraph (as was truly the case). To this, one man is heard to murmur: "The President himself knows how to do these things, while he drinks his chocolate in [the presidential palace of] Chapultepec."[17]

In all the editions subsequent to 1893, Frías repeatedly alludes to the soldiers as victims of "duty," implying that the Díaz dictatorship obliged its troops in the name of duty to carry out atrocities against the mountain rebels. Thus the author makes clear his idea that both the *tomochitecos* and the conquering *federales* were victims of a system that fed on injustice in the name of a hypocritical abstraction.

Finally, Frías alludes, in a somewhat veiled fashion, to what may have been hidden causes for the revolt itself. While pondering the question of the Saint of Cabora, in whose name the townspeople of Tomochic had rebeled, Mercado asks himself whether perhaps she had been only "a very fine istrument, a crystal, operated in the shadow by hidden hands."[18] Furthermore, the hero asserts that the initial defeat of the batallion was "a disaster for which others were to blame," and that there was "something sinister in all that."[19] But when the time comes to single out conspirators or manipulators of the rebellion, Frías can do no more than throw out such sly hints; it is doubtful that he had inside information at any rate.

Only by the time that the 1906 rewriting took place was Frías ready to see, in retrospect, that the spirit of revolt might well have spread to other parts of the country—as in 1906 it indeed had. In view of Frías' opposition to the Díaz regime, it might be thought that he advocated such a contagion in "the other peoples of the *sierra* who suffered from a somber malaise ready to resolve itself in rebellion,"[20] but in fact, he speaks otherwise. On this point post-revolutionary critics have erred in attempting to establish Frías as a champion of rebellion, as one who saw the Tomochic campaign as a prelude to liberation. The truth is that in 1906 Frías still saw the revolt for what it was: a tragic encounter between ignorance and arrogance and a "horrible war of Mexicans against Mexicans."[21] At the mere thought of widespread uprisings, Frías expresses an honest horror: "For a moment the sublieutenant tried to imagine what might have been in Chihuahua, in Sonora, in the entire republic. . . . How much useless bloodshed, then, what a national catastrophe to the benefit of ambitious, of hypocritical bandits who would trade their *chilapeño* hats of backwoods uprisings for a top hat at state banquets."[22]

IV The Military Ideal

While it was certainly a tragedy to Frías' country, this grisly little campaign also meant a very real calamity for the author, because the military had previously signified for him an ideal. While still studying at the military academy at Chapultepec, he became thoroughly imbued with admiration for the military virtues of bravery, skill, and loyalty. The actualities he found in battle, however, by no means lived up to the lectures of his academy professors, and it is the resulting disillusionment that Frías expresses through his hero Mercado which provides a principle theme of the novel.

Tomochic, even while showing that paradeground commanders are ineffectual in battle, goes a step further in revealing a conflict in Frías, own attitudes toward the myths and realities of armed warfare. The fact that Frías is fascinated with military life is evident throughout the novel (and other works, as we shall see) in his detailed accounts of battles and in his constant eye to detail in picturing the soldier's life. Prior to the campaign, Frías' total military experience had been confined to the barracks and the paradeground. The realities of the expedition, therefore, held a fascination for him, even though they turned out to be both enlightening and bitterly disappointing.

Frías had, as a young cadet, turned to the army for personal acceptance and moral values that he had not found as a civilian. Even as a soldier in Mexico City, he had repeatedly succumbed to the bohemian habits he had acquired at an early age, and because of his retiring nature he did not find acceptance by his companions in the barracks. So it was to the rigors of warfare that he looked in his search for something—a group, a set of values—worth pinning his life to.

It is not his officer peers, however, but the anonymous Mexican soldier who ultimately receives most of the novelist's attention. In *Tomochic* we see him in nearly all aspects of his life: marching, talking, singing, drinking, suffering defeat, and celebrating victory. Herein lies the relatively limited *costumbrismo* of his work, for while Frías happily refrains from treating the soldierly life as picturesque or quaint, it is clear that he considers this mode of existence to be closer to the virtues he sought than those of higher status. If not always the hero he should be, the common soldier at least embodied an admirable stoicism, as one trooper glumly comments that "they'll kill us anyway. . . . It's just walk and walk . . . and then die like goats!" (p. 12).

In a masterful and chilling chapter entitled "Los perros de Tomochic" ("The Dogs of Tomochic," written and published initially as a separate short story and added to the novel in the 1906 and 1911 editions) Frías paints a fine word picture of a soldier: " . . . the old soldier, a Oaxacan of good stock for cannon fodder: soul tempered in long and hard sacrifice, round and darkly bronzed face; narrow, stubborn forehead, prominent cheekbones, sparse and bristly hairs on his chin; sinewy neck and stubby body, robust and agile. He stood facing [Mercado], good-natured and attentive. Poor sergeant, perhaps he would never return to his beloved land to the South!" (p. 111).

Still, regardless of his deep sympathy and admiration for the uniformed Mexican, Frías speaks always with the distance of an observer, not the intimacy of the sharer, as he writes of Mercado, who can only feel at home in the company of soldiers when he is drunk. Symbolically, Frías' conflicting attitude is embodied in three soldiers—Mercado, his friend Castorena, and Captain Molina—and in the revealing contrast they present.

Mercado is the idealistic youth who goes into battle with illusions of glory, loyalty, and valor such as are rarely found outside of epic poems, textbooks, and other sources of myth. But where he expected (or hoped) to find courage in himself, he finds only fear—a cold, brutish terror that tells him to drop his rifle and run. Only another fear, that of being caught in an act of cowardice, restrains him. Around him, in his first neck-jerking test with reality, he sees "vanished all of the high ideals of his life; not even the solemn poetry of war remained intact! War as he had thought it to be, as he had read of it: grand, noble, heroic, epic!" (p. 79). Far from baring his epic soul, warfare brings out the bestial underpinnings of his nature. This occurs not once but three times, all just after the heat of battle:

Water, water! . . . Miguel saw the water and fell upon a ragged woman who was defending herself from a group of soldiers who were asking for some of it, some begging, others threatening. [. . .]
"Out of the way! Out of the way! What the devil is going on? A peso for the jug! Look, here it is," and he showed the lady four quarter-peso notes.
"Ay, Sublieutenant. . . It's for my man who's real bad off! Let me have it sir, and I'll bring you some later. . . ."
Ignoring this, he grabbed it from her ferociously, throwing her the bills. (pp. 77-78)

On another occasion, Mercado obtains food, a half-cooked piece of meat: "The blood trickled between his avid lips. He held the reddish lump with both hands, chewing with loud smacking noises, like a savage. He could have bit someone if they had tried to take it from him" (p. 78).

Finally, after the ultimate defeat of the insurgents, Mercado, drunk, mounts a horse and gallops through the smoking ruins, a frenzied and bestial incarnation of Cataclysm as he shouts "Long live death!" (p. 133). Thus the experience of war is seen to have wrung the humanity out of Mercado, leaving a thing sometimes less than human, seldom more than monster: a soldier.

Castorena, or *"Sesos de Bronce"* ("Bronze-brains") represents another facet of soldierdom. He carries no idealism into battles; his only concern, wherever he is, centers around wine, women, and song. No concept of glory bothers this warrior, much less respect; he is not even above robbery, pillage, and sacrilege: "A beautiful Tomochic hen, roasted in the fire of the burning church! What a tasty dish!" And Castorena smacked his lips" (p. 53).

It is only in the fury of combat that Castorena becomes admirable. His own ferocious nature takes strength in the melée and carnage, and he assumes the role of leader to the disoriented riflemen, "sublime," as Mercado sees him, "in the noble ire he displayed" (p. 62). Castorena is the wartime soldier, a misfit in the barracks, a disgrace on the drill ground, a clown on payday, but magnificent in those moments when war's savagery matches his own.

Standing in contrast to both Mercado and Castorena is Captain Molina, who is Mercado's idea of the exemplary military man: "so worthy, so enthusiastic, so thoughtful, so candid; he who discussed the Napoleonic battles with such ecstasy" (p. 104). Gallant leader, expert tactician, and fatherly, though demanding to his troops, Captain Molina dies in an attempt to save a wounded *Tomochiteco*. This irony causes Mercado to realize that glory and honor have no place on this unholy battlefield and that death comes as hideously to the hero as to the coward.

As he makes clear in later writings, Mercado's disenchantment was Frías' own. His interest in military affairs, curiously, did not die: his *Episodios militares mexicanos,* the *Biblioteca del niño mexicano,* and *La vida de Juan Soldado* are among many of Frías' later proofs of his sustained fascination with soldierdom. Nevertheless, it is noteworthy that in these works Frías will write with a clear knowledge that the soldier's life is a brutish one and that the needle of armed glory, if it is to be found, must paradoxically be sought for in the haystack of wanton cruelty, chaos, and stupidity that are the true essence of battle.

V *Style and Nonstyle*

The plot and structure of *Tomochic* is simple and direct. Its chapters are short and episodic, as was inevitable in a novel written to be serialized in a newspaper. (This and other matters link *Tomochic* with Azuela's *Los de abajo.*) Yet whatever else is said about this work must take into consideration its evolution, as the 1893 chronicle was reedited by its author in 1894, 1899, 1906, and 1911.

The first edition, as noted before, is found in the pages of *El Demócrata* between March 14 and April 14, 1893. The second edition, like its predecessor, is anonymous and contains numerous, though relatively minor, changes in the text. Printed in Río Grande City, Texas, by Jesús Recio, it also contains many errors. In its 1899 third edition (Barcelona: Maucci), *Tomochic* for the first time claims Heriberto Frías as its author and shows evidence of considerable rewriting, mainly in more fully developed descriptions and narration, as well as considerably more detail concerning the rebellion. The fourth edition, printed in 1906 by the Casa Editorial de Valadés (Mazatlán), is further expanded to the point of including two entirely new chapters. The last edition prepared by the author, by Bouret of Paris, appeared in 1911 and is identical in text to the fourth. This edition was again made available in 1951 by the Editora Nacional (Mexico City) in a facsimile edition. Finally, *Tomochic* was reedited in 1968 by Porrúa (Mexico City) as number 92 of the "Colección 'Sepan Cuántos,' " with prologue, notes, and some textual editing by James W. Brown.

The thread of the story is identical in all, though some minor factual details are altered; for example, the earlier editions claim that "Mercado" had been in the army only two months prior to the campaign, but the fourth and fifth editions change this to two years, which is true in Frías' case. Also, some dates and names are altered in the later editions. Very possibly these had been falsified in the earlier versions to conceal authorship of the novel; then later, when the Tomochic campaign was no longer a sensitive political issue, Frías presumably rectified these details and added his name as author.

Much more significant, however, is the evolution of the novel's style as evidenced in sharper descriptions, better use of vocabulary, smoother transitions between episodes, more dialogue, fuller character delineations, and more frequent shifts from an omniscient narrative to interior points of view. We have already noted that the later novels also contain greater criticism directed toward the government. These differences between the first and final editions of *Tomochic* are, in fact, so substantial that literary and historical judgments concerning *Tomochic* cannot ignore them. To be fair to both Frías and his novel, only the later editions should be taken in literary judgment, while those interested in historical scrutiny of the events brought about by the novel's first appearance should direct themselves to that first edition. The interim editions are of interest in showing how the novel evolved. Possibly because the first, second, and fourth editions are rare, critics have not taken this comprehensive view of *Tomochic*'s peculiar nature. Such limitation is typified by J. L. Read's reference to the 1899 edition when he dismisses Frías' insufficient "verbal equipment" and adds that "the style is journalistic, fairly well composed, but inelastic and without sparkle."[23]

The characters portrayed in the primitive editions are truly skeletal. Particularly in the first and second editions, Miguel and Julia receive scant psychological detail, while minor characters get practically none at all. Miguel remains in a one dimensional romantic outline as a thin, melancholy, warmed-over imitation of Werther, Goethe's great romantic hero. In later versions, however, significant realistic details make him more acceptable to the literary palate. The stress of battle and his affair with Julia are now connected with inner conflicts, his indecisive nature, and his aimless search for personal worth.

Julia, too, changes from romantic silhouette to at least bas-relief with some shadings. Throughout, she retains her basic features as an innocent and submissive damsel, resigned to her sordid existence with the "ogre" Bernardo, but in the later versions she is more believable, still a bit cloyingly fawnlike, but with certain habits that mark her as rustic and even ignorant, such as a convincingly irritating habit of repeating "Oh, how silly of me" in awkward moments. Her "trembling hands" become "beautiful, strong hands," which are far more likely in a girl who spends mornings splitting firewood. In general, she becomes less fragile and more appealing. Contrasting her characterization in the 1894 and in the final editions makes clear that Frías' descriptive and evocative powers later became sharper and depended less on romantic cliché. The 1894 version reads: "In those moments she raised large, dark eyes, and her glance seemed to express melancholy and resignation, as if comprehending the somber fatality of her destiny" (p. 26), whereas the later description is: "He saw her cross the room, graceful and pure, among nauseating rags, and in one moment when she lifted her head with birdlike grace, he saw shine toward him the timid and sweet magnificence of her black eyes" (p. 20).

Curiously, while the main characters tend basically toward a sharpened realistic flavor, their love affair, which Azuela noted correctly as a useless digression, becomes more romantic in the final versions due to the author's filling out passages and scenes with emotive padding.

So while the novel's major figures improve, as does the novel's story in general, there is also a noted increase in attention given to the minor characters, such as Cruz Chávez, Bernardo, Captain Molina, and to nameless soldiers, mountaineers, and *soldaderas* (camp followers), who appear only briefly but stand out with the sure stamp of individuality. Such deft, quick characterizations are already Frías' *forte* and will carry him well in later works such as *Los Piratas del Boulevard* and *¿Aguila o sol?*. They also anticipate the often-praised *brochazos* (brush strokes) that mark the Azuela style.

Frías foreshadows Azuela, too, in his use of dialogue—at least in the final version—as a faithful reproduction of the popular speech, pungent and barbed, that is every common Mexican's heritage and joy. José Ferrel notes that Frías' characters are so earthy that "in their words there beats a nationalism of the purest spontaneity," that they often remind the reader of some old friend, long absent, "and whose encounter now makes us stop to shake his hand and ask him where he has been."[24] Frías' contemporaries could not, or would not, strive for such effects.

Nor could they (or would they) shake the reader with the sights, sounds, and smells of battle in passages that mix romantic pathos with lucid, stark realism, as this strikingly montagelike scene:

> . . . and the first enemy bullets began to whistle from below, between the trees. The battle was beginning.
> The officer prepared his carbine, trembling, waiting to see the Tomoches whom he felt there hidden, and who were stepping up the fire. Their shouts grew, savage shouts that gripped the troops who were desperate, unable to see their adversaries, unable to advance or retreat, obliged to accept combat on such unfavorable terms.
> The thick air wrapped itself in white smoke, of a strong and acrid odor. . . .
> Behind the heavy fog of gunpowder beat, in brief reddish flashes, the muzzle discharges.
> At each moment the shouts grew louder, clearer, and the enemy bullets, with better accuracy, had sharper whistles, beginning to pass head high.
> "Long live the great power of God! Long live the Sacred Trinity!" were the shouts and cries that the breezes carried to the soldiers, sometimes very distinctly.
> One, mortally wounded in the chest, opened his arms, dropped his Remington, and whispering painfully an "Oh my Jesus," fell a cadaver, head down, vomiting blood. He was the first victim. (P. 58)

This is characteristic of the fuller detail added to later editions: swift-paced, vigorous, bold in tone and color. These and other improvements are so extensive as to put in doubt López Peimbert's assertion that the novel does not change basically in style; the fact is that the alterations that occur between the first and fifth editions make clear that the former are little more than drafts of the latter. As the novel improves, the narrating voice of the author recedes into the background at crucial moments to leave the characters' own voices, actions, and thoughts to speak for themselves. Thus the chronicle becomes the novel.

Frías' vocabulary or "verbal equipment" also moved toward precision and a greater use of movement, color, and sound as "scorn" became "horror and revulsion" and "enemy bullets" became "hail of steel." However, he also continued to insist on "infinitely sad," "glacial breezes," and similar romantic stock phrases.

A further element that the final editions develop with greater depth is *costumbrisma*—the depicting of characters, types and customs in their particular milieu. The greater part of this centers around army life, as we have observed. Except for fixing his attention on the life and lot of the Mexican soldier, Frías shows brief interest in local color aside from details useful to the story. Certainly, it would be incongruous in a novel such as *Tomochic* to dwell upon the local inhabitants as being quaint or picturesque (as did Frías' contemporaries), and fortunately Frías does not attempt to do so. Instead, he ennobles the valor and strength of the northern mountaineers without hiding the fact that their customs sometimes appall him. The same may be said of the soldiers, whom he admires at times, pities at times, but always keeps at arms' length. The ragged, raucus gangs of camp followers, or *soldaderas,* too are depicted in fine detail as they care for their fighting consorts, but Frías confesses frankly that they inspire in him a mixture of "tenderness and terror" (p. 28). Typical of Spanish and Spanish-American *costumbrista* writers until very recently, Frías' stance is that of an outsider, a bemused observer, even though Frías is more clear-eyed than most and refrains from the pious sermonizing that other nineteenth century novelists, such as López-Portillo, Rabasa, Altamirano, and Gamboa, were prone to.

In sum, the occasional abuses that gall the modern reader, even in *Tomochic*'s later versions, detract, but bearably so, from its unifying fabric of vigor and unabashed authenticity. Now rapid and brutal, now ponderous and sentimental, the novel is admittedly uneven, but in it the author breaks loose surprisingly often from current literary fashion to express his chaotic vision of a young soldier caught up in a struggle that he scarcely understood and of a cancerous society that Frías himself fought to fathom. *Tomochic* reflects, in a very real sense, the same unlettered majesty found in old epic poems, whose rough harmony and unsubtle masculinity have usually eluded the more learned poets. In his own grumpy way, Azuela gave eloquent tribute to this quality by declaring that "*Tomochic* produces a sensation of relief and rest from so much honeyed and bloated literature that is passed off on us with the name of novel."[25] Frías' urges were, from the very outset, epic; but he was yet to find a cosmic struggle of which to sing. In *Tomochic* there was no hero to enshrine, no virtues to uphold. The villains were distant; the forces of evil, vague, diffuse; and even the victims were foul and surly. Frías the author is seen casting about for a True Cause that will sort out the forces at play. He finds none, and Mercado is left confused, self-pitying, an unwitting harbinger of twentieth century antiheroics, spiritual isolation, and incommunication, which Frías would not have cared to see as "modern" so much as simply distressing.

CHAPTER 3

The Other Novels

I *Why Novels?*

THE reader is reminded that Frías did not seriously consider becoming a novelist until after he had written *Tomochic* and was told, quite to his surprise, that his "chronicle" was a novel. At this point Frías (whether he actually realized it or not) faced a problem. *Tomochic*'s first primitive edition found popularity through its revelation of Díaz' bloody and blundering expedition to the North, not for its limited literary merit. Now, if Frías was to continue as a novelist, he would have to learn his trade. Could he do it? In his favor was a fiery temperament, a sharp and critical eye, a devotion to truth and candor, a deep and almost primitive faith in justice, and a life that had already seen sadness, tragedy, and outrage, all material aplenty for novelistic expression. Unfortunately, Frías also had liabilities: his education was spotty, his sense of outrage was not always matched by his feel for style, his health and habits were erratic, and he was living in a period of Mexico's history when proclaimers of truth found life difficult, to say the least.

Frías recognized or sensed his problems as a beginning novelist, for he wrote and rewrote his first three novels over a period of years. *Tomochic* underwent changes in 1894, 1899, and 1906; his next novel, *Naufragio (Derelict)*, written in 1895, was completely rewritten in 1908 and published as *El amor de las sirenas (The Love of Sirens)*, and his novel of 1896, *El último duelo (The Last Duel)*, was polished and republished in 1907. Furthermore, if we are to believe a statement in his 1916 *Miserias de México (Miseries of Mexico)*, a primitive version of this work was written around 1900 but never published.[1] It is apparent that Frías saw shortcomings in these novels and attempted to improve them, as indeed he did. However, just as his life was a long series of pendulum swings between fame and misery, so too was his artistic production uneven in quality, ranging from brilliant to banal.

Why did he continue writing novels? A prime motive must have been money. Frías often complained that he was driven to write like a machine simply to support himself and his family, to supplement his income as a reporter and journalist. But more importantly, Frías burned with a messianic spirit to strike out with his pen, to flagellate with the truth, to punish with his wit. To this ex-soldier, the desktop was now his battleground and the printing press his artillery.

In addition, the very type of novels that Frías wrote shows that he considered them closer to his soul than the rest of his voluminous output. Within his great preoccupation for the truth, Frías' favorite subject—himself—is treated in his novelistic works with a humility and forthrightness that quite nearly approaches the catharsis of confession. Unlike essays, articles, and short stories, which Frías also wrote prolifically, novels gave him an opportunity to speak at length about himself, to exorcize his personal demons. He missed no opportunity to weave himself into his novels, even those which are not openly autobiographical. Frías is always there in one or another character, as we shall see.

II The Love of Sirens

Frías' second novel appeared in 1895, in the pages of José Ferrel's newly reopened *El Demócrata*. First called *Naufragio (Derelict)*, the much improved second version appeared in book form as *El amor de las sirenas (The Love of Sirens)* in 1908. A subtitle to *Naufragio* was *Los destripados (The Dropouts)*, and both title and subtitle referred to students who, seduced by the siren call of idleness and vice, leave their studies to join Mexico's legions of pimps, thieves, and charlatans. Thus the title *El amor de las sirenas* also connotes the multiple temptations of drinking, vice, narcotics, and gambling that contributed to the downfall of young university students. In the introduction to the second version Frías says: "I too was a dreamy bohemian who, head in the clouds, found myself wallowing in filth, burning with brief flames, swept by changing winds, heroic and visionary at times, scandalous and unseeing at others, sincere always, wasted, and finally, by work, love, and misfortune, condense from my own blood, into these ramblings, a near autobiography."[2]

In this novel, which is excellent in many respects, Frías demonstrates his ability to portray the intimate lives of Mexico's urban middle class. Much of the action takes place in a Mexico City tenement dwelling, anticipating Mariano Azuela's later *Nueva burguesía (New Middle Class)*. The various apartment dwellers are memorably described in a microcosm that includes two spinster sisters who make pastries for a meager living, a drunken and profane Spanish widow, railroad workers, a shoemaker whose wife shrieks nightly from the pain of neuralgia, washerwomen, seamstresses, and an old man who incessantly saws out the same Italian tune on his violin. Contrasted with these drab souls are several students who call themselves the *Club Provinciano* ("Provincials' Club") and who gather nightly to drink and carouse.

The president of this group and protagonist of the novel is Pedro Santiesteban, a medical student noted for his intelligence, his appeal to women, and his comparative wealth. Reared on a country ranch in Chihuahua, Pedro came to the capital a model of health and clean living, only to be slowly corrupted by his associations in the city. Another major character is Federico Argüelles, or "Papá Argüellitos," the erratic mentor of the group.

At first Santiesteban is an outstanding and popular student. His small group of admirers freely celebrate his wit and prowess; he in turn pays for their interminable sprees. Soon their influence begins to tell upon him, and he turns egotistical and prideful. Against the advice of his companion Argüellitos, Pedro begins to abandon himself to heavy drinking and easy romantic conquests. One object of Pedro's pursuits is Lupe, a pious and attractive ex-servant girl who was once forced into marriage and does not wish to submit to Pedro's advances. Pedro is at first impressed by her virtue in resisting his advances and even momentarily feels a chaste devotion for her. Soon, however, he renews the attack, and Lupe submits. The pair live in carnal bliss for three days; then Pedro tires of her and turns elsewhere.

His next target is Isabel who, being rich, worldly, and haughty, offers an intriguing challenge to Pedro. But Isabel is no easy conquest; she is an experienced seductress who prefers to reel in her own victims slowly. When finally they become lovers, Pedro abandons his studies, and the two disappear to a rented cottage on the city's outskirts. With a thousand-peso check that Isabel has given him, Pedro finances an orgy that continues for days, then weeks.

The lovers do not leave the house for fear of being seen together on the streets, and in their hideout they leave no sensuality untasted. Isabel, experienced and insatiable, initiates Pedro to every facet of refined decadence, from the Modernist verses of "Duque Job,"[3] to either inhaling and worse.

Pedro, reduced to semistupor, offers no objections when Isabel suggests they go to Cuba. Once in Havana, a free-wheeling city, they submerge themselves deeper still in unbridled vice. Before long, Pedro is so addicted to all its forms that his health begins to crumble. Isabel, tiring of her partner, leaves for New York, while Pedro, left penniless in Cuba, supports himself and his addictions by selling pornographic literature and drawings. He is often kept by prostitutes for his somewhat withered charm and his skill in injecting morphine.

Santiesteban's friends in Mexico City are unaware of his whereabouts; they only know that he has left his studies and that the police are looking for him, because Isabel's thousand pesos were stolen from her uncle. As a further complication, Pedro's sister and his aged father, concerned, have traveled to Mexico City to seek him out. Lupe and Argüellos, to save them the grief of an unexplained disappearance, claim that Pedro is away on a trip to assist a famed surgeon. Unfortunately, the white lie fails when a local woman comes to Lupe's apartment and drunkenly exposes Pedro, relating his faults in the most vivid terms. The father overhears and is thunderstruck. Unable to bear the shock because of his advanced age, he dies soon after. Pedro's sister enters a convent.

With matters turning tragic, Pedro enlists the aid of a prostitute who returns with him to Mexico. His state now is one of advanced degeneration; he is a haggard, shaky derelict, with a puffy face and open sores. When he reappears among his friends and tells them something of his recent activities, Lupe becomes fired with the hope of saving him through her self-sacrifice. She then surrenders to the police, declaring that she stole the thousand pesos, and so while Pedro undergoes the horrors of morphine withdrawal, Lupe serves his jail term for him. Even though Pedro's friends continue to give assistance, they openly despise him for what he has become. Lupe, too, learns all about Pedro's moral decay from a prostitute, so she gives him up as a lost cause and, when released from jail, agrees to marry Argüellos, who truly loves her and longs for the love and care of such a woman. Pedro, on the other hand, recovers his health but keeps his unwholesome habits. The novel ends as he departs for Guadalajara, and Argüellos observes wryly that they represent "the Mexican middle class, neither good nor bad, but . . . capable of either" (p. 477).

III   The Last Duel

The subject of Frías' next novel, *El último duelo, (The Last Duel)* was inspired by the famous Verástegui-Romero duel that shocked Mexico City in 1895. Felipe de la Serna, of the newspaper *El Imparcial*, was a hidden witness to this duel and caused a sensation with his published account of the event—so great, in fact, that public indignation put a legal end to such "affairs of honor" in that same year. Frías novelized the events leading up to the incident, though he placed the time of the novel during the brief presidency of Manuel González (1880–1884), "to follow with them," says Frías, speaking of the fictitious characters, "in this story the course that events took, as happens in life, in this embryonic society of ours."[4] Though nominally a piece of social criticism directed at the practice of dueling, which increased greatly during the first years of the Díaz period,[5] the dominant note of the work is its scathingly satirical picture of the capital's new-rich bourgeoisie and of the self-serving and sensationalistic press.

The principal characters are Luis Borostia, a young historian and dueling instructor; Joaquín Montiel, a wealthy rancher and devoted family man who had won honor leading guerilla troops against the French, although he has since fallen into bad company in the big city; and "Don Chucho," Jesús Rabas, who in league with his seductive wife Amelia runs a profitable extortion and blackmail racket.

The novel begins at a dinner party held at don Chucho's home. Attending the gathering are numerous "notables" of the city whom Frías deftly describes as tasteless, greedy, and vain. The movement of the crowd and the colors, odors, and snatches of small talk that emanate from it are memorable:

> With a sugary and effeminate voice, twittering coquettishly, he was saying:
> "Oh heavens! How this life agrees with Don Chucho; fatter every day, and every week a new pair of pants. And do you know where he sends them for tailoring?
> "To Salín? Where else!" said one of the so-called ladies, fanning herself.

"Not Salín, Licentiate; to the Baratillo [a slum], right? exclaimed the other 'lady.' "

"Not at all, Juanita, to Sarre [a stylish district]."

"Yes, to Sarre, where Don Joaquín gets dressed . . . and Amelia gets dressed—and undressed—at Madame Anciaux's place . . . where Don Joaquín's daughter gets dressed—and undressed. . . . It's all the same, isn't it?" (1907 ed., p. 5)

Suddenly, angry words flare up between Amelia and Montiel. He had believed that they would be alone tonight, but she has arranged a large dinner party. Seeing Montiel abuse Amelia, Borostia calls Montiel a coward, and the latter knocks Borostia to the floor. The incident is reported in the papers the following day, in sensational and lurid descriptions that promise a duel. But both Borostia and Montiel would be ruined by such a scandal by admitting their affairs with Amelia. Montiel would sacrifice his family's good name, while Borostia, who has dueled before, would be breaking a promise made to his mother that he would never duel again. Yet with the threat of being publicly branded as cowards, neither of the principals dares back down.

Borostia's fiancée Isabel and Montiel's daughter Josefina make frantic attempts to bring peace and finally wrest a promise from both men that they will not duel; but just as the sordid matter seems settled, one of the city's newspapers launches a series of insinuating and insulting articles. Others take up the cry, each attempting to outdo its rivals in sensationalism and all demanding a duel. The city's appetite for violence is whetted, and coffeeshop idlers and gossips everywhere demand bloodshed. Borostia mysteriously loses his job, and the president openly questions Montiel's once-famed manhood.

Montiel goes to Amelia's home to break off with her and to remove himself from her grasp. She retaliates by telling him, untruthfully, that the author of the articles most insulting to him is none other than Borostia himself. Outraged, Montiel challenges Borostia. The latter accepts, even though his fiancée leaves him and his mother dies of grief. The duel, the climax of the novel, takes place as a somber and tragic event that terminates in great suspense and drama:

"Attention!" shouted the general. "One! . . . Two! . . . Three! . . ."

The combatants' arms outstretched. There was a dry detonation in the great silence of the fields . . . and Luis, who had not fired, nor even turned to face his adversary, dropped his pistol, and his arms crossed, shot in the temple, fell face down, biting into the mud. (P. 264)

IV The Triumph of Sancho Panza

In his next novel, *El triunfo de Sancho Panza* (*The Triumph of Sancho Panza*), Frías returns to the semiautobiographical novel and revives Miguel Mercado, his novelistic alias. This story takes place in Mazatlán, where Frías lived in 1906–1909, and deals with life there and with Mercado's ultimate flight from that seaside community. In the novel the author portrays various types of social predators that he encountered there: "The rascally, grasping lawyer, a master at intrigue; the rapacious and daring financier; the bold professional. . . . The weakness of the sentimental, of the lyric ones, dashed to pieces, and . . . only practical, common sense and cold reason together with self-interest can triumph: Sancho Panza" (Introduction, p. 1).

Mercado, disillusioned and humiliated by his repeated defeats in the practice of journalism in Mexico City, is offered and gratefully accepts a position in Mazatlán as editor of *El Faro*.[6] *El Faro* is a nonpolitical newspaper, and Mercado eagerly looks forward to an escape from the tumultuous and corrupting political scene. The lush seacoast climate strengthens and revitalizes Mercado; he is delighted by the beautiful women and the passionate young men, and he is entranced by the local customs and traditions. Soon, however, Mercado begins to realize that he has not yet reached paradise, as he observes the furious competition between families to see their daughters named queen of ceremonies during spring festivities, and as he notes social pressures hounding both rich and poor.

Mercado also identifies a parasitic element in the city that has found a likely victim in Manuel Muileón, a rich engineer recently arrived in town. He is simple-minded, innocent, and childish—a perfect victim: ". . . sawed-off, negroid, chubby, almost obese. His face was a doll's with sideburns, and out of his thick Chinese style mustache smiled a childlike mouth; his bulgy and ugly myopic goggle-eyes peered from behind glasses (p. 47)." Among those who have conspired to unburden Muileón of his wealth are Pedro Santiesteban (protagonist of *The Love of Sirens*), who carries on an unlicensed medical practice between amorous episodes; Licentiate Mercurio, a shyster lawyer; and Mr. Orland Fields, an American professional swindler. María, Muileón's frivolous wife, is caught up in a flirtation with Santiesteban, and through his influence has persuaded her husband to settle in Mazatlán. With Santiesteban as a close friend of the family, he, Mercurio, and Fields ensnare Muileón in a spurious business venture designed to drain him of his funds.

As Mercado becomes aware of the plot against Muileón, he feels a desire to warn the intended victim, but he knows that in doing so he would make powerful enemies and jeopardize his peaceful existence in Mazatlán. So he prudently decides to remain silent. Then one night Santiesteban proposes that Mercado write a series of articles favorable to the venture in exchange for a share of the spoils. This shocking proposal brings to a head the conflict between Mercado's ideals and his desire to avoid strife. Should he give in to self-interest as Sancho Panza might, or should he risk all to see justice done and very likely end up as a very battered Don Quixote? His experiences of recent years tell him not to fight with windmills, but he is now faced with becoming part of the conspiracy itself. The decision is difficult, but Mercado takes his stand for Don Quixote. He writes an article denouncing the plotters and exposing their scheme. Unfortunately for him, the "ingenuous Knight of the Sorrowful Pen"[7] misses his mark. No one believes such outlandish accusations; townspeople brand Mercado as a liar and slanderer for having struck out at such upstanding citizens, and Muileón, not comprehending the warning, angrily brings charges of libel against Mercado, who loses his editorship of *El Faro* and is forced to flee with his family from Mazatlán. Having lost everything in a fruitless sally against corruptive power, Mercado reflects bitterly: "Back to Mexico City, you miserable hack, you who thought yourself a protector of other peoples' affairs; go back poorer and older to your miserable life of a pen-pusher, until you croak some day, from fatigue and sorrow" (p. 231).

V   Miseries of Mexico

The next novel, *Miserias de México (Miseries of Mexico)*, fills in the hiatus in Frías' autobiographical novels between *Tomochic* and *El triunfo de Sancho Panza*—the period between 1894 and 1906. Since this novel is almost entirely autobiographical, much of what transpires in it has already been recounted in this study, but by way of telling his own story, Frías draws an engrossing though depressing picture of Mexican journalism at that time and of the pitiful life of newspaper writers, forced into degradation and servility.

Miserias de México traces "Miguel Mercado" from his departure from Chihuahua enroute to the capital soon after his court martial to his unceremonious exit from that city twelve years later. At the beginning, the ex-lieutenant's idealism is almost boundless, as he dreams of becoming a crusading journalist and writer: "He dreamed deliciously that as he hung up his sword, which was not virginal, like so many others', and after breathing the smell of gunpowder and blood in a fierce campaign, it befitted his high mission to continue, pen *en guard,* on the road of Truth and Liberty" (p. 5).

The realities of journalism in Mexico City turned out, however, to admit few honorable warriors. His first position consisted of merely clipping news from other papers and of writing favorable or unfavorable comments about important individuals according to whether or not the personage in question had bought his proper quota of subscriptions.

Mercado begins to drift from one newspaper to another, only to find that all are essentially the same. Unable to accept such a state of affairs with the stoicism or indifference that his fellow workers seemingly have, he seeks solace in alcohol. Not many months later, Mercado is deep in the grip of alcoholism and at twenty-two years of age presents a pitiful image of a man. Now subject to fits of hysteria, the young writer slides from job to job as each successive editor is less willing to hire him. Then follows a four month stay in a hospital, after which Mercado finds himself all but unemployable. He turns to morphine and, under the stimulation offered by this drug, cranks out a stream of free-lance articles, novels and historical works. Soon however, the "siren" morphine has drained him of all moral fiber and personality, and he can no longer function at all.

Just as he is all but dead, a young widow, "Fina," encourages him to enter a hospital. So just as before, in Chihuahua, a woman intercedes with fate, and Mercado is saved. Two months later he is released and marries her, determined to reform and remake his life. Not surprisingly, his reputation as a drunkard and addict makes job hunting difficult. Working as a lowly proofreader and later as a reporter, he barely keeps his wife and himself from starvation, and so he attempts to supplement his earnings by writing articles, pamphlets, and even circus advertisements on order. Nevertheless, he steadfastly refuses to indulge in the journalistic blackmail that provides financial support for many of his companions, "starving hacks who, though bearing no grudge, must raise a fuss to give life to their pages, and also to themselves" (p. 39).

Mercado's redemptive wife falls ill, and he is obliged to look for a more lucrative pursuit. After trying unsuccessfully to gain a position in a ministry, he finally turns to the theater. Believing naïvely that his yet untried talent as a playwright will place the city at his feet and bring him the funds that he so desperately needs, Mercado composes a short musical farce. Then, after months of work and weeks of rehearsal, the luckless writer watches from backstage on opening night as the play fails disastrously.

By now twelve years have passed since the ex-hero of Tomochic arrived in Mexico City eager to become a journalist and champion of truth. Now, defeated and publicly humiliated, Mercado accepts the editorship of a small newspaper in faraway, sleepy Mazatlán. Just three days after the play, his last hope of glory hissed out of existence, Mercado flees Mexico City.

VI Heads or Tails?

¿*Aguila o sol?* (*Heads or Tails?*), Frías' last published novel, is quite different from the others. Here is a warmth and contemplative spirit very rare in his previous novels. Here, too, Frías presents a broader epic view of Mexican society at the brink of her great and terrible revolution. This novel's protagonists are Gaudelia Ramos and Miguel Mercado, representatives of the "Mexican Woman" and the "Mexican Journalist," to whom the book is dedicated. Of Mexico's women, Frías maintains that "she has suffered and still suffers, more than the Mexican man, the sorrows and miseries of her race, her homeland, and of her home, because she, as mother, sister, friend or daughter of the combatant, encourages him, inspires him, purifies him, and forgives him" (Introduction, p. ii). Then, in his dedication to the Mexican journalist, Frías proclaims that "the journalist will be in essence the future hero: The educator, the propagator of useful, good, and beautiful truths, willing to suffer all in order to know all, willing to burn in order to illuminate" (Introduction, p. v).

The symbolic Mexican woman, Gaudelia Ramos, lives with her aunts in a small village called Mixtlán. They belong to the poorer and outcast branch of the powerful Aguila family of landholders who trace their origin back to colonial Mexico. Gaudelia's branch of the family, however, has been oppressed and persecuted for generations by their wealthier relatives, and the girl's aunts barely get by, and are reduced to selling candies and pastries for a living. Gaudelia has grown up an outcast, too. Forbidden entrance to school for being "unruly," she leads a carefree existence singing in the streets, caring for other urchins, and protecting the village's stray animals. A kindly priest gives her some education, but more importantly, she is naturally endowed with grace, talent, kindness, and (to the rage of her rich spinster cousins) beauty.

As a child Gaudelia dreamed of becoming a saint, but as she approached womanhood she decided on a simple, secular life of good works. As her first notable act of piety, she set to converting an American cattleman known as "the *gringo* heretic" to the Catholic faith.

This man, Hanssen, has designs on Gaudelia, but they are of the most honorable sort: he hopes to see his son Alberto marry her. A mixture of practicality and idealism, Hanssen envisions a new "breed" combining the virtues of the two races, like the hybrid cattle for which he is well known.[8] But Gaudelia, a romantic and passionate soul, feels little attraction to Alberto, since he is logical, reserved, and a little boring, surely not the type for "desperate romance," such as she has read about in books by Jorge Isaacs, Gustavo Adolfo Béquer, and Manuel Flores.[9] Nevertheless, the two become unofficially engaged, oblivious to the envy and gossip of Mixtlán's feminine population.

At this point, Pepe León Aguila, son of the landholder "Anselmo the Rooster," comes home during school vacation, to the delight of the town's legion of eligible girls. This dissolute semi-intellectual, the latest of the Aguila dynasty, finds the local girls all too facile, so he turns his passions to Gaudelia. Much to his surprise, he receives a sound slap and a bloody nose for his efforts, so he retires to sulk and write dreadful sonnets.

Now the action follows Pepe back to the capital, where he renews his efforts to break into its intellectual inner circle even though he is actually only a pompous, drunken playboy. His crowning achievement—and his downfall—is his sponsorship of a banquet in honor of the dictator. The affair is an incredible phantasy of political and literary personages, an "apocryphal banquet." Miguel Mercado, one of those attending, observes the gallery of personages and catches bits of conversation up and down the dinner table, like this one (referring to Francisco Madero, soon to be president, and to his famous book *La sucesión presidencial en 1910*, which did so much to bring down the Díaz regime): " 'Crazy Panchito' is a journalist from San Pedro de las Colonias who is also writing a book, a very amusing one according to his uncle don Ernesto; it's called 'The Next Presidential Succession' " (p. 183).

Utilizing this scene, the author describes or typifies almost every important figure in Mexico of that period. Then follows an outrageous after dinner speech by Pepe León Aguila in which he toasts the glories of Porfirio Díaz in a grotesque glorification of decadent Positivism: ". . . the empire, our empire, has pygmies at its feet . . . [pigmies] who want land, water, and justice and who only deserve the yoke, pepper, beans, and *pulque;* and against whom we must fight . . . with the whip" (p. 200). All the while, Miguel looks about him and asks himself what is to become of Mexico in the perilous years ahead.

A patriotic celebration is meanwhile being planned in Mixtlán for the upcoming holiday. Gaudelia, famed for her voice, was to have sung, but her vengeful cousins have had her barred from performing. The town council, looking for a substitute, writes to *El Imparcial*, a leading Mexico City newspaper, asking that they send an orator for the occasion. So it happens that a few days later Miguel Mercado, fortyish, near-sighted, and plump, descends from the train at Mixtlán.

Mercado, a habitual observer, wanders through the village streets, chatting with workers, elders, and shopkeepers. In the process he comes to know the history of the area and of the two warring factions of the Aguila family—the rich and conservative Anguilas and the poorer liberals, Gaudelia's forbearers. Mercado also meets Gaudelia and feels revitalized by her fiery spirit and patriotism. Once again he falls under the spell of Don Quixote and decides to discard the bland celebration speech he is expected to give and instead to speak out against the feudal oppression that enslaves Mixtlán both politically and economically. Since he sees in the hamlet a "symbolic but alive, hot, sick and, infected condensation of the Mexico of that time" (p. 241), he determines to risk one last charge at the windmills.

So in his celebration address, heard by the entire population, Mercado delivers an oratorical history of Mexico's sufferings, with broad allusions to Porfirio Díaz, the national dictator, and to his local counterparts, the Aguila family. The rich in the audience are horrified, but the poor applaud wildly. Then amidst the uproar, Gaudelia appears on the stage and begins to sing of patriotism and revolution. The howling masses are brought to order only by the cocked and pointed rifles of soldiers.

As news of the scandalous event spreads throughout the republic and revolution appears yet more imminent, Mercado makes another hurried escape, but this time his exodus is that of a hero, punctuated by a warm and fraternal goodbye between Mercado and Gaudelia, the Mexican journalist and the Mexican woman incarnate.

It should be remembered that ¿Aguila o sol? was meant to be the first installment in a trilogy on the Mexican Revolution, but Frías did not live to write the other two. Doubtless he intended to follow "Mercado" (himself) through his stormy years of the constitutional convention, his trial and imprisonment under Carranza, and on to more peaceful—though not always better—days beyond. Thus a potentially memorable and vividly personal history of Mexico, encompassing the Díaz era and the revolution as well, was interrupted by the author's death and will forever remain incomplete.

VII *Analysis and Comparison of the Novels*
A Characters

We can see now that all of Frías' six novels are to a greater or lesser extent recountings of Frías' own life. *Tomochic, El triunfo de Sancho Panza,* and *Miserias de México* are frankly and openly so, while *El amor de las sirenas* leans heavily upon Frías' bohemian experiences; further, the character "Papá Argüellitos" is without doubt a mask of Frías, as can be seen in a number of ways: a description of Argüelles (p. 10) matches Frías' appearance and personality; they both have a long history of alcoholism and drug addiction, with frequent stays in the Belén Jail; and Argüelles is given to long tirades reflecting Frías' opinions, and even talks often of preparing a book to be called *El amor de las sirenas*. Miguel Mercado appears, too, in the novel, though indirectly, as the characters talk of him. Once it is mentioned that he hopes to marry, if only he can reform as his "sweety" *(amorcito)* demands. A friend says: "Can you imagine the poet Miguel, the hero of Tomochic, without his grimy hat, without his rundown shoes, with his hair combed, clean collar, and sober?" (p. 145). Later, friends say that he is married and settled down, where he "waters his garden, listens to his thrush, and feeds his chickens" (p. 469).

El último duelo makes the character Borostia into Frías' image as an ex-officer of the army, a young man with a hopeful career in journalism and also an author of Mexican military engagements, as was Frías. Also, *¿Aguila o sol?* derives from Frías' speeches in support of Diego Redo in Mazatlán (hence the "Mixtlán" of the novel) that precipitated his untimely flight from that city on the eve of the revolution (even though, as we shall see, the novel's plot actually derives from Emile Zola's *Germinal*).

In addition to the author's masks, other stock characters reoccur, such as the rustic but honest provincial, as a wholesome embodiment of the simple life. Often this person comes to the city and becomes corrupted, as do Joaquíin Montiel of *El último duelo* and Pedro Santiesteban of *El amor de las sirenas*. Another character is the "redemptive woman."[10] Just as Frías found deliverance in the person of such women throughout his life, his characters also seem often to encounter women willing to sacrifice in order to save others; such are Julia of *Tomochic*, Lupe of *El amor de las sirenas*, and Gaudelia of *¿Aguila o sol?* Still another personage is the *catrín*, or dandy, the dissolute Santiesteban, Pepe León Aguila, the lawyer Mercurio of *El triunfo de Sancho Panza*, and other such gaudy predators for whom Frías had special loathing.

In general Frías' characters perform a Dickensian function as types and figures. Uncomplicated by subtleties of personality, they serve only to support the allegory in which they move; thus as personalized characters they may seem unidimensional and overdrawn, but as allegorical beings they are convincing, even masterful. So also are minor figures—such unabashed caricatures, especially in *¿Aguila o sol?*, as the brutish major don Pepe Márquez, or the super-Catholic "Rosary Sisters" who inhabit wakes, funerals, and deathbeds, dressed always in black, "their flags of mourning" (pp. 100–101).

Frías' apparent lack of creative ability in the production of rounded characters is offset by his well-developed powers of observation, cultivated no doubt by his journalistic calling. Where he fails to create characters, he reproduces vivid portraits of those whom he has known, sketching them in bold strokes and firm lines, though with little shading. We know them by their actions, by some salient aspect of their appearance, or by their speech. Frías' verbal portraits

The Other Novels

are among the best in Mexican literature; "they breathe," as José Ferrel says, "a thick air of reality and remind us of individuals and types we have met in real life."[11] But graphic as these likenesses are, they are static, unsubtle, and incapable of the complexity, surprise, or independence that human characters, fully drawn, must have:

trying to be clever, the obese barrel-man gave his puffy, shining face, red and idiotic, the beastly expression of a Hottentot idol. (*El último duelo*, p. 7)

as they listen, a scrawny little man—pock-faced and sawed-off, almost dwarfish, yellowish hair, beard and skin, a gray bowler wadded half onto his head, lively little cat eyes—almost simultaneously and with grandiose gestures, chatters, smokes, drinks and laughs. (*El triunfo de Sancho Panza*, p. 35)

B Structure and Style

Simplicity of plot line is also characteristic of Frías' novels; only rarely did he depart from a simple chronological sequence of events. Flashbacks, subplots, and alterations in the ordering of events require much care and planning on the part of the author, and it is apparent that Frías was rarely willing to take such pains. *El triunfo de Sancho Panza* and *Miserias de México* simply narrate the author's own life from one date to another; they might better be classified as chronicles than novels. *Tomochic*, in its latter editions only, is embellished slightly by two flashbacks, the chapters "La derrota de la segunda columna" ("The Defeat of the Second Column") and "Tomochic se prepara" ("Tomochic Prepares Itself"). *El amor de las sirenas* contains a fairly conventional flashback at the outset, as does *El último duelo*.

¿*Aguila o sol?* stands apart in the matter of structure. Written as it was after Frías had retired from journalism and politics to the calm of a diplomatic post in Cádiz, this last published novel is Frías' most mature work. It incorporates two story lines (one concerning Gaudelia and the other Mercado) that fuse only shortly before the final scenes. The fascinating though rambling "apocryphal banquet" scene is also a sudden though perplexing departure from his customary simplicity. Though it does not advance the plot at all, as a literary device the banquet recalls the *cēna* (banquet) of Roman satirists, through which the writers displayed and criticized ostentation, bad manners, and poor taste,[12] all of which are displayed in abundance by Aguila and certain of his famous guests.

Although Frías generally concentrates on people and devotes comparatively little time to surroundings, he occasionally turns a painter's eye to physical settings, especially in evoking the senses: "The room shone white with cleanliness: the wood floor, just scoured by the scrublady's stiff brush, shimmered, while little wool curtains hung over the doors to soften the intense morning suns; the brass bed's rods stood out like gold around the rose-colored mattress; the white marble top of the bureau glittered, and in the basin atop the metal washstand the clear water, smelling of bichlorate, spoke of antiseptic rigidity" (*El amor de las sirenas*, p. 45). Often his descriptive passages show the bombast of Hugoesque Romanticism, as for example this depiction of a seashore: "The eternal din of the water was an eternal lullaby to the writer's meditations, as it shattered against the dike or exploded against the reefs and crags, a clamor . . . now languid and whimpering like begging, now grown potent and magnificent with thunderous detonations of raging surf, with the vast rumble of angry hordes" (*El triunfo de Sancho Panza*, p. 51).

Typical of Mexican literature of that time, Frías' novels contain a crossbreeding of Realism and Romanticism. No doubt Frías' own personal circumstances contributed to this mixture, for in spite of his sentimental and passionate disposition, he was devoted to truth and accuracy, which were held as ideals (in lip service at least) by Mexican journalists and Positivists alike. Frías fervently believed in the power of truth, but he, like Emile Zola (who was also a journalist), could never be detached and objective, as befits true Realism. His novels seethe with moral indignation and sentimentalism. His characters are not random, average subjects who appear to govern themselves in the manner of a Realistic protagonist. They are unusual or exaggerated types who inevitably come to represent a vice, a virtue, or a viewpoint. They seem to exist in order to "demonstrate" something.

Frías' writing underwent few basic changes during his first years as an author. His first publications are stiff and written in a monotonous third person. Confusing bombast and strained rhetoric for good style, he insists on trembling hands, pale faces, exclamations such as "Oh!" and other overused devices. His works dating from 1893 to 1910 gradually show fuller descriptions, a greater surety of vocabulary, and more dialogue, but are the same declamatory admixture of Romantic emotion and Realism throughout.

Los piratas del boulevard (1910) and subsequent works show a trend toward shorter, surer sentences with less declamation and overblown lachrymosity. At times, Frías appeared to anticipate the unadorned brushstrokes of Mariano Azuela's later Realism in such passages as the following:

> Sun-stroke and exhaustion. A man tired and fallen, a dead man. The officer drives the sword point into the human beast's neck, draws it out and wipes the blood staining the steel upon the blackish shirt of the cadaver. . . . "It'd be dangerous for the sick or crippled to give information to the enemy; you got to finish them off." (*La vida de Juan Soldado*, p. 8)

> They didn't get mixed into politics. . . . They gambled their guts and their hearts like real men, over a drink of *mezcal*. "Put up or shut up, sonofabitch." (*¿Aquila o sol?*, p. 215)

> "Begging your pardon, but my cousin Anselmo is just a barnyard rooster. Even he says that he only crows in his own corral. At the Mezcalera hacienda there's lots of *pulque* and liquor and lots of chicks and hens. And he likes all that so much, Mister President!"
> "Is he a big drinker?" asked the Caesar.
> "No sir. He's a big drunk."
> "Then he's not very dangerous."
> "And also a gambler and womanizer."
> "Then he's no good at all." (P. 113)

Such crisp, sure scenes are rarely found in his earlier works, but they grow common after 1910.

Also, the later writings show a greater expression of warmth than Frías had permitted himself before. Mercado himself can be seen in *¿Aguila o sol?* as a kind and fatherly figure, still sentimental, but no longer in the emotive Esproncedan manner. He can now speak of himself (i.e., Frías) without tears or clenched fists—" 'Semipoet, semi-impulsive, semisincere, semihero, semidrunkard; neither fish nor fowl', professor, just an imaginative, listless, sentimental nobody' " (p. 228)—whereas in previous works he was inclined to enunciate: "Alone! . . . What a sinister word! It summed up all the affliction of his unfortunate life; it held the bitterness, the disenchantment, the infinite tedium to which he would be perpetually condemned!"[13]

The best yardstick of Frías's evolution in writing style is to be found in *Tomochic*, since there we can see his changes of technique as the author wrote and reworked his best known novel in 1893, 1894, 1899, and 1906.[14] A noteworthy improvement in style (and tone) is apparent on close examination, and it can rightly be said that the first and second editions are little more than rough drafts when compared to the third and fourth.[15] The following passage in its various stages shows how dramatic the alterations often were:

Make it tequila; I don't like sotol, and he gave a twenty-five cent bill to Julia, who approached timidly. He noticed her, moved by the irresistible grace of the damsel so brutally mistreated by the old man. He vaguely glimpsed the deep suffering that lay hidden in that den shared by a bear and a gazelle, and he thought of his own family misfortunes with an infinite bitterness. (First ed.; *El Demócrata*, March 15, 1893, p. 2)

"Make it tequila; I don't like sotol," and he gave a twenty-five cent bill to Julia, who approached timidly. He noticed her for her irresistible grace of a damsel so brutally mistreated by the old man. He vaguely glimpsed the deep suffering that lay hidden in that bear's den. (Second ed., p. 25)

"Make it tequila; I don't like sotol," and he gave a twenty-five cent bill to Julia, who approached with timidity. He noticed her for the irresistible grace of a damsel so brutally mistreated by the old man. He vaguely glimpsed the deep suffering that lay hidden in that bear's den that reeked of tobacco and sotol. (Third ed., p. 35)

"Make it tequila; I don't like sotol," and he gave a twenty-five cent bill to Julia, who approached with timidity.
And he contemplated with astonishment and surprise the rare grace of the young woman, so brutally mistreated by the old man. Who was she? . . . Where had she gotten such beauty? He envisioned atrocities in the dark bear's den that reeked of tobacco and sotol. (Fourth ed., p. 19)

In this passage, Frías progressively moves more and more to the background, leaving the character more opportunity to show his thoughts himself. He also removes the reference to his own life, which was irrelevant; he sharpens the allusion to the home ("bear's den," "reeked of tobacco and sotol"), and in the final edition he leads the reader to wonder—as does Mercado—about Julia, alluding to "atrocities" rather than the vaguer "suffering," and questioning "Who was she? . . . Where had she gotten such beauty?" Thus the chronicle becomes a novel.

The Other Novels

Throughout his career, Frías adhered to certain words of Romantic overtone, among them "woeful" *(tristisimo)*, "choleric" *(colérico)*, fateful" *(fatídico)*, infinite *(infinito)*. René Avilés points out Frías' "schoolboyish use" of adjectives, but is fair enough to remind us that this was the accepted style of his time.[16]

C Costumbrismo

Very closely intertwined with the depicting of characters is the element of *costumbrismo:* the representation of local lifestyles and customs (with a preference for the quaintness of rusticity or local color) that figured in many Spanish and Latin American writings of the nineteenth century. Frías, the eternal observer, wove his impressions into the novels that he wrote, as well as into other works that we shall discuss later. We can truly say that Frías reproduced local types and customs with a "painter's eye," especially if we think of him as an Impressionist who sought to catch the momentary flash of colors amidst the play of moving sights and shadows. Tomochic's most memorable word pictures are of this sort. They set the pattern for Frías' life-long interest in military life and in the lower classes. Of the first, Frías' youthful fascination for the clash and glitter of soldierdom turns to bewilderment, then to horror as the campaign progresses; but even so the author seems transfixed by the soldier's life (he would always remain so) and appears obligated to record his impressions of its every aspect:

> At four in the morning on the next day, October twentieth, the soldiers were silently roused. In the mountains, at that hour and that time of year, it is still blackest night, the deep darkness and the cold are intense.
>
> They spoke in whispers. In the darkness it seemed like a coming and going of specters. The first sergeants of the company did not call roll but only counted the rows. Those who had been on perimeter defense rejoined their respective sections. In the starlight could be seen, from close up, pale faces, trembling chins and dry lips under the hoods drawn tight. (pp. 53–54)

Tomochic sees the soldier marching, resting, drinking, starving, bragging, trembling, killing and dying: "Some soldiers saw from behind the trees and rocks how, finally, the young captain raised his carbine and tried to raise up and fire; but he fell face down with his mouth open and foaming, biting the mountain pebbles, seeming to embrace them with his open arms in a final tragic convulsion" (p. 65).

With equal fascination, Frías pictures the women who accompanied the troops, the *soldaderas* who formed a noisy mob of thieving harpies in the mass but cared for their men with dogged loyalty: "In the burning horror of the march, they carried on their high mission of mercy, defying the cudgels of the corporals and even the officers' swords to deliver water to their thirsty companions, who through their black Indian eyes of resignation showed their gratitude with the ecstasy of appeased thirst" (p. 11).

Frías' interest in the *soldaderas* and the semibarbarous inhabitants of Tomochic extended, in later works, to the poor throughout Mexico. Writing of the urban poor in Mexico's Baratillo district, Frías underscores the filth and squalor that prevailed there: "It was an awful hodgepodge of blankets, straw hats and shawls, a stomping about over slime of *pulque* and urine. . . . The soppen glory of Xochitl amidst twentieth century Mexico—street vendors, barefoot prostitutes—*pípilas*"—looking savage with their faces smeared with rancid oil, harpies, *soldaderas*—not even tolerated in the barracks, yelling abominations and epileptic obscenities (*El amor de las sirenas*, p. 440).

¿*Aguila o sol?* is a particularly rich tapestry of local color, from the local landholder's frequent sallies among the tenant farm girls, to "old don Pablito the Harpist, seated in a corner, who officiously sang barracks ditties, sad ones full of love and hate, rhymed by the wailing melodies of his ancient harp" (p. 245).

Finally, it is the journalist's existence that also runs its costumbristic thread throughout Frías' novels. Even when deploring the newspaperman's lot, Frías shows a thinly veiled pride when describing the uproarious parties, the witty conversation at a café table, the romantic, self-styled bohemianism that Frías shared like a cloak of honor with his tattered colleagues, and the heady atmosphere in the newspaper office itself, where ink bottles and papers shared table space with tacos or bottles of *pulque*, and the air reeked of onions and ink.[17]

Long after interest has died down in the specific events that Frías described in his novels, and when Frías himself should in time fail to attract readers as an historical personage, the graphic and vivid glimpses of turn-of-the-century Mexico will stand out in these novels with a warmth and color that time will not easily erase. It is here that Frías' works represent an important layer in the archeology of Mexico's past.

CHAPTER IV

Other Works of Frías

TO think of Heriberto Frías only as a novelist and journalist is to overlook his other diverse and important works. Frías' widely varied experiences, and often his urgent financial needs, brought him to court all manner of literary forms. He composed poetry, on and off, practically all his life. His keen interest in the military life brought forth not only his novel *Tomochic,* but also *Episodios militares mexicanos* (*Mexican Military Episodes*). *La vida de Juan Soldado* (*The Life of Juan the Soldier*), and many articles and poems dealing with soldierdom. With his powers of observation sharpened by years as a newspaper reporter, Frías produced a series of social satires known as *Los piratas del boulevard* (*The Pirates of the Boulevard*), "Miserias de México,"[1] "Cáscaras y semillas" ("Peelings and Seeds"), and many individual articles that depicted with remarkable clarity the types and customs of his day. Acting as a collector and popularizer of pre-Columbian legends, he composed still other works, such as *Leyendas históricas mexicanas* (*Mexican Historical Legends*). He also wrote short stories, many of which mirrored the polished frivolity of the popular Modernists such as Manuel Gutiérrez Nájera. Finally, he wrote dramas, of which we have only his own descriptions since they were never published and have been lost.

Many of Frías' nonnovelistic works seethe with the same frankness and vitality that sparked his better novels; others are pale imitations of current literary fads or, worse yet, suffer from the hurried writing of a hungry and driven author. Nevertheless, Frías' nonnovelistic writings are quite deserving of study, not only for their literary interest but for their historical content as well.

In order to examine a broad sampling of these works and to present a representative cross-section of Frías' kaleidoscopic and voluminous output, the following categories will be utilized: historical works, contemporary satire and short stories, and poetry and drama.

I *Historical Works*

A Mexican Historical Legends
For this collection of stories, Frías turned to Mexico's Indian past, declaring patriotically in his opening remarks that the roots of the Mexican past should be within the reach of all her people.[2] The first edition of this work was published by Librerías Ediciones Andrés Botas in 1899, with successive editions appearing in 1931 (Antigua Librería Robredo) and in 1957 (Editora Nacional), all in Mexico City. They are all identical except that the last edition omits the author's introduction.

The *Leyendas históricas mexicanas* actually have their origin in the newspaper *El Imparcial* of 1897 and 1898. They first began to appear in November 1897, inauspiciously printed on the newspaper's last page, though soon they moved to first page status with accompanying illustrations. Appearing under the lead titles of *Páginas nacionales* ("National Pages") or *Episodios históricos* ("Historical Episodes"), they were read for nearly a year in *El Imparcial's* Sunday morning editions along with news of the Dreyfus case and the United States' war in Cuba. Late in 1898 they began to appear less regularly and were soon replaced by the *Semanas alegres* ("Pleasant Weeks") of the *costumbrista* Angel de Campo.

In its book form, *Leyendas históricas mexicanas* is divided into two parts: the "Leyendas históricas" ("Historical Legends"), dealing with Indian history prior to the Spanish conquest, and the "Cuentos históricos nacionales" ("National Historical Accounts"), which contain episodes of the years immediately following the downfall of Tenochtitlán (Mexico City at the time of the Aztecs). In all, the book consists of forty-five narratives, thirty-seven in the first part and eight in the second.

Ordered in a loosely chronological form, the series begins with the arrival of the Tenochcas, ancestors of the Aztecs, in the Valley of Mexico and follows their rise to power through centuries of struggle, until their defeat and collapse under the Spaniards. As the stories progress, the events also broaden to include other cities and tribes. Thus as the Aztecs establish their hegemony over central Mexico, the episodes begin to incorporate the life of Netzahualcóyotl, fabled philosopher-king of Texcoco, and subsequently include legends belonging to the Mixtecs and Zapotecs of the South.

As a popularization of Indian history and customs, this series is written in a highly readable and entertaining manner. Each story contains detailed descriptions of customs, celebrations, dress, religious ceremonies, and daily life. Such practices as human sacrifice, ceremonial warfare, self-mortification, and competitive selection of kings are fully described.

The stories center for the most part on themes of warfare, revenge, mystery, and fate. "Solgluna" ("Sun-Moon"), for example, begins with a vivid description of a sunset over the twin volcanoes Popocatéptl and Ixtaccíhuatl as the cruel and haughty emperor watches from his palace, convinced that the heavenly show of colors has been staged expressly for his pleasure. Then night begins to fall. The emperor contemplates the melancholy stillness of the two mountains, "the Guardian Warrior" and "the Sleeping Lady," and summons to him an old priest, a prisoner from Mitla: "Tell me, Old One . . . . Why do those giants never rouse, and why . . . in the blackness of the night are they like terrible phantoms? . . . What were they? . . . Tell me. Tell me their story, wise priest . . . and you will return to Mitla laden with offerings for your great palace-temple-tomb" (pp. 51–52).

Now the priest relates the story of the two mountains. In life, they were the first man and the first woman to walk the earth in their Garden of Eternal Flowers. Their creator Tlaque Nahuaque intended that they should stay in their garden-paradise, but pride and curiosity led them to forget their rightful place, so they began to wander about the earth, living in caverns and caves, seeding the world with their offspring. Forbidden to return to their valley, they wandered for ages in search of rest and shelter. Finally they came upon a valley of great beauty and chose to die there. Ixtaccíhuatl lay down as Popocatéptl stood guard over her, and there they remain, forever frozen by Tlaque Nahuaque as an example and warning to their children who inhabit the valley that all must be humble before the gods and obey their commands. To this parable the old priest concludes, "Listen well, emperor, or woe to you. Look hence. Meditate. Mend your ways." Then, as the moon spreads its white rays over the palace stones, the king shatters the silence of the night with an order shouted to his guards: "Let this old Zapotec die of hunger!" (p. 54).

Another story that equals the previous one in its dramatic atmosphere is "El paraíso guerrero" ("The Warriors' Paradise"). The Aztec noble Tlalnahuitl prepares himself for holy warfare, for conquest and glory. Priests and seers have predicted that his fame will be everlasting, and his soul will gain glory and immortality for his deeds. But amidst the fanfare and ceremony surrounding the army on the eve of its departure, Tlalnahuitl is troubled by a dream in which his lover has appeared to him, dead. The anxious youth consults a wise and venerable priest and recounts the dream. The wiseman responds with joy. Yes, he says, it is true: two virgins have indeed left the holy convent; one was destined for the king's harem, and the other has been sacrificed to go to the Warriors' Paradise, from where her spirit will guide the youth to glorious battle and perhaps even to a holy death. Then the fortunate youth will join his lover at the feet of the god Huitzilopochtli in eternal ecstasy. The priest describes the bliss that awaits the soldier, whereupon the latter, impassioned now, exclaims that he will now go gladly to battle to kill, to take prisoners, and to join his beloved, Xilitl, in death:

"Miserable one, what did you say?" roars the priest, taken by sudden rage. "Do you love her?"

"With all my heart. And she will be my wife."

"Be damned, blasphemer! She is now the king's wife. May justice be done. Everyone! Come at once!"

... And for such audacity the noble youth was put vilely to death ... and his spirit went not to dwell in the kingdom of the heroes but to shadowy Mictlán, the red and black hell, for the one he loved was the king's woman. (Pp. 109-14)

These stories, dramatic to the point of being declamatory, may actually be closer to a reproduction of an historical scenario than an objective or scholarly description of the time. Mariano Picón-Salas has noted in his essays that these people were possessed of a lyrical sadness and that their view of existence was marked by "fatality and catastrophe."[3] Certainly these stories of Frías' reinforce such a view of the Indian character, as much as do, for example, the strange and haunting remnants of aboriginal Mexican poetry and song that we may still read and ponder.

The form that Frías utilizes in his *Leyendas históricas mexicanas*, that is, the short dramatization of historical episodes, is derived from a popular literary vogue of his day, one initiated by Ricardo Palma in his "Tradiciones peruanas" ("Peruvian Traditions"); Palma was widely published at that time in Latin American periodicals and newspapers, including the prestigious *El Mundo Ilustrado* and *La Revista Moderna* of Mexico City. Basically, Palma's formula consisted of embellishing a historical incident with whatever fictitious material he felt was needed to make good reading, much in the manner of present-day historical novelists. There were in Frías' day several Mexican imitators of this style, among whom were Enrique Olavarría y Ferrari, E. Maqueo Castellanos, René Maiseroy, and Luis González Obregón. Frías lacks the chatty style and good-natured humor that mark Palma's still-popular "traditions," but he compensates with his heady aura of dark mystery and powerful passions, especially in his swift, jolting climaxes.

Frías, unlike the other writers of historical fiction just mentioned, turned his talents to Mexico's Indian history, and to this degree his pieces may be considered an abrupt departure from the usual. In other parts of Latin America, the Indian had already become a favorite theme of numerous authors, but Díaz' Mexico was nearly devoid of Indianist literature in its fervor to emulate Europe.[4] True enough, there were histories of pre-Columbian Mexico, and good ones, but not until after the Díaz era was the Indian widely considered to be a fit subject for artistic expression. Ciro B. Ceballos, in an essay on Frías published in 1902, echoed the "refined" literary taste of his day by saying that Frías, though dedicated to the truth, was "without instruction" and that he had "much to learn," doubtless meaning that he did not write in elevated style, nor did he populate his stories with Greek and Roman mythologies (as did Ceballos) and that ". . . his myopic visions have not yet discerned in the enchanted garden of art, the carbunculous pupils of the Minervine bird that announce the glimmer of the flashing helmet of the goddess who watches over us wretches who carry under the dome of our cranea the burning candle of the idea. . . ."[5] Let the reader judge!

More realistically, J. L. Read states that "this series of stories is basically poetic in conception. The haze of atmosphere of a strange land of strange peoples . . . blends with the phantasy of physical nature to make a harmonious interpretation that is more poetry than prose."[6] The exotic and often dreamlike ambient that Frías uses and his use of such Nahuatl words as *teocalli* (pyramid) and *huipilli* (Aztec cotton dress) induce Read to classify Frías as a "Modernist writer."[7] While granting that grandiloquent flourishes and the lush background that characterize these stories give them a tone that might be termed modernistic, they lack the elegant serenity and static grandeur that grace the modernistic treatment of exotic themes. They bear far more resemblance to the Romantic writers of Spain, such as Zorrilla and Espronceda. It would be reasonable to suggest that just as the medieval past was the favorite inspiration for Spain's Romantic writers, so the Indian past was here utilized by Frías. The atmosphere of the *Leyendas* is at times quite poetic, as Read correctly observed, but it is turbulent "poetry," mysterious and violent, often approaching a nightmarish fantasy similar to the mood of Espronceda's *El estudiante de Salamanca (The Student of Salamanca)*:

> Frightful visions, terrible shadows, shadows of fantastic giant women crowned by great, high headdresses of fire, bodyless heads flying hellishly in a reddish atmosphere, among bloody hearts crowded in a compact mass, like a sea of scarlet waves. (P. 115)
>
> The hurricane of killing, the horrible, savage wantonness of slaughter came to an end . . . and then, in the silence of the great and bloody lakes and in the lonely and shattered forests, there blended the dreadful elegies of the wounded, writhing in the shadows, with the delicious song of the thrushes. (P. 149)

Much patriotic pride enters into Frías' interpretation of Aztec life. The dwellers of *Anáhuac*, the Valley of Mexico, are not so glorified as were the Romantic era's "noble savages," but they are portrayed, even in their baser moments, as being above all else vigorous and proud. We see in them the same steadfastness that evokes the author's praise in *Tomochic* and elsewhere. Thus the primitive Tenochcas, when persecuted and pursued into the swamps of Lake Texcoco, exemplify the warlike tenacity that was later to build an empire, as ". . . instead of the cowardly emotion of their misery and a life of execrable slavery, the people felt martial stirrings and warlike desires!" (p. 15).

Frías' picture of the Aztec's spirit and energy as they fought their way to independence and eventually to power serves well to heighten the later tragedy of their downfall and their return to slavery and shame at the hands of the Spaniards; he writes that "those unhappy souls were stripped by the thousands of their liberties, of their families, of their goods, and of their country, to go under the landholding master's whip, to cultivate for him the lands which belonged to the Indian himself, sweating blood of humiliation, weeping tears of fire" (p. 301).

In view of such sympathy for the Indians—a recurrent theme in *Tomochic, Miserias de México, ¿Aquila o sol?, Episodios militares mexicanos*, and elsewhere—it is reasonable to believe that Frías saw in the aboriginal past the seeds of his country's present suffering. Frías sought in the history of the Aztecs and of their neighboring tribes a symbol of Mexico's soul. While other writers were craning their necks toward Paris and London, Frías kept his eyes on the Mexican soil and found there not only cause for pity, but also a source of pride. Both of these views of Mexico—a deep sense of tragedy and intense patriotism—are eloquently expressed in the *Leyendas históricas mexicanas* as elsewhere in Frías' words.

B Mexican Military Episodes

Frías' introduction to this two volume work is dated October 1900. The two parts are subtitled respectively *Guerra de Independencia (War for Independence)* and *Invasión Norteamericana (North American Invasion)*. Included in both volumes are numerous maps, portraits of military leaders, and other illustrations of battle scenes and soldiers in action.

Part One of *Episodios militares mexicanos* is concerned with the military actions against the Spanish during the War for Independence. Since it omits all aspects of the war that are not tactics, battles, and troop movements, this work is not a complete history of the war. The years of political infighting and the conditions that precipitated the war are not here; neither are such events as Hidalgo's final retreat and capture, Morelos' *Congreso de Chilpancingo* (Chilpancingo Congress) and his betrayal and death, and even the actual winning of independence, by political intrigue, under Iturbide—all these are omitted.

Once again Frías reveals his patriotism in this historical series, as he dwells on the common Mexican's heroism—not only of soldiers, but also of women and even children—in the heat of battle. One such incident tells how a boy, *El Pípila*, braved Royalist bullets to set fire to an important fortification during the battle of Guanajuato. Still another describes the valor of a youngster who singlehandedly managed to fire a cannon into an advancing column of Royalists during Morelos' defense of Cuautla.[8]

Part two of Frías' *Episodios* deals in much the same manner with the North American invasion of 1846–1847, for the author again ignores the complex politics that surrounded the war. Chronologically, the volume begins with Taylor's invasion of Palo Alto and ends with the fall of Mexico City. Its most noteworthy chapters are those describing Zachary Taylor's attack on the unsuspecting and ill-prepared Mexican army near Guerrero; the battle of Angostura, after which Santa Anna ordered an unnecessary and disastrous retreat even though he had not lost the battle; and the heroic defense and martyrdom of six young cadets who defended the National Military Academy's hastily erected fortress against the advancing Americans. As in the first volume, Frías takes great care to underscore the bravery of the common soldier and Mexican citizenry against overwhelming odds from without and incompetent leaders within.

Manifest in all the *Episodios* is the military training of their author; the battles and campaigns are discussed from a tactical or strategic point of view, and each encounter is analyzed to bring out major military errors or successes. Surely Frías was remembering the classes he had attended at the Military Academy when he penned such lecturing passages as these:

> Here we should observe that Allende was lost by his lack of foresight as he naïvely believed that a veteran such as Calleja would set off without first reconnoitering the plaza and taking . . . all the data necessary about its state of defense and location of the troops stationed there, so as to attack at the weakest point. ("La toma de Guanajuato," I, 85–86)

> Add to this the fact that, through carelessness or lack of time, the prime action of clearing the terrain in front of the fortification, cleaning out the trees, was not carried out. ("Monterrey," II, 46)

> . . . now we shall see a truly magnificent military operation, bold and well planned, precise and tactical, carried out by an inexperienced general, but, for that, yet more admirable still! ("La retirada del Saltillo a Zacatecas," I, 106)

Troop movements, defense positions, and battle plans are all minutely described, including enumeration of units, armaments, and supplies. The reader who knows something of these matters doubtless is in a better position to enjoy the *Episodios*, but the awesome fascination of warfare also comes through, as Frías' obsession with the military life would lead us to expect: "Terrible on their tall, black Frisians, the American dragoons charge upon the guerrillas, but as they close, the guerrillas wheel their horses swiftly; the agile Mexicans dodge the mighty Yankees and take them from behind, raining blows with machetes on their backs, their necks, wherever they can" ("Episodios Aìslados: Las Guerrillas," II, 255).

Seeking to awaken patriotism, Frías envisioned that his *Episodios* would be read by officers to their troops, by fathers to their sons. He was convinced that in those days of much-touted peace and prosperity, few citizens were aware of Mexico's debt to the common Mexican soldier, "who, if well led and encouraged, goes soberly and tranquilly, bravely and boldly, wherever his leaders take him, to victory or to death . . . or to both glories perhaps!" (Introduction, I, 9).

A gauge to Frías' precarious state in 1900 at the completion of this work is the fact that in it he entoned hosannas to the very dictatorship he hated. Declaring in the Introduction to Part One of his *Episodios* that the book was to be a "homage to his [Díaz'] campaigns for the final peace called progress," Frías dedicated it to the "President of the Mexican Republic, Citizen General Don Porfirio Díaz" (I, 5). At this time, Frías was seeking a way out of the direst poverty and persecution, but to little avail; the Díaz government never forgave Heriberto Frías for his past transgressions. Perhaps it could read between the lines and see that the occasional passing remarks about corrupt clergy and incompetent presidents and generals could be read in the present tense; that in speaking of "these Indians who yearn to shake off old, shameful and abominable yokes" (I, 9), the "general suffering of the oppressed people" and "humiliation brought about by privileges and honors given to European outsiders, and all the pent-up desires to be free and sovereign on the land that their forefathers plowed" (I, 20), Frías was actually making thinly veiled references to the present state of affairs. It is little wonder, then, that he remained persona non grata in "respectable" circles until the dictatorship's long-awaited end.

Frías style in the *Episodios militares mexicanos* can best be described as declamatory. As the author meant the *Episodios* to be read aloud, they bristle with bombastic outbursts meant to capture a listening public.

And, oh, the unfortunate Allende, the brave and upstanding champion full of heroism and loyalty, full of sacrifice for his great ideals, was shot in the back . . . as a traitor to his country! . . . He, a traitor? . . . What sarcasm! ("La batalla de Calderón," I, 101)

Everything was failing badly! . . . Was it the end? Ah, no! . . . ("La Explosión Inicial," I, 17)

Everything was failing badly! . . . Was it the end? Ah, no! . . . ("La Explosión Inicial," I, 17)

This sort of declamation, common in Frías' time, may now seem ponderous to the reader and even evoke an indulgent smile, but Frías manages it well, especially in the battle scenes, where bombast is less out of place and where Frías own memories of the din of armed struggle give vivid life to the narrative: "And meanwhile the clamor is frightening and colossal; and anguished is the cry of those on the rooftop, besieged, spewing fire, death, blasphemies, heroism, and lead; while from below come waves of stones, arrows, and spouting rage with each exploding grenade, each stone or enormous beam that plummets down, bounding with crashes of cataclysm, opening skulls and bellies in that dense human mass!" ("La Toma de Granaditas, I, 40).

Lacking depth in the portrayal of personalities, it is the "human mass" that emerges most memorably. Dialogue and individual portrayals are seldom encountered, and the human voice is heard almost exclusively en masse in the roar of battle cries. Even such historically important persons as Hidalgo, Morelos, and Santa Anna are not presented in detail but appear as vague figures at the head of their troops. Although Frías tells us that Hidalgo was of an uncertain and vacillating nature, or that Rayón was bold and daring, unfortunately the author of the otherwise engrossing *Episodios militares mexicanos* does little to draw human portraits of Mexico's most famous military leaders or to remove the dull green patina of park statuary from our memories of them. But Frías' life-long preoccupation with the Mexican masses again surfaces in these *Episodios,* as elsewhere, as does the bronze, restless horde that was soon to mold the Mexican Revolution. In this regard Frías was most prophetic, far more so than he could have realized.

C Books for Mexican Children

Closely related to the *Episodios militares mexicanos* and the *Leyendas históricas mexicanas* is this series, *Biblioteca del Niño Mexicano,* published in 1900 by Maucci and comprised of one hundred ten small booklets of about sixteen pages each, with illustrations in color; in other words, strongly resembling in format the "dime novels" that were popular at the same time in this country.[9] The illustrations themselves give an accurate impression of the stories, for they are dramatic and exaggerated, with bloody scenes of battle and heroically posing generals, all, we can suppose, meant to attract the young reader's eye. Likewise, the stories themselves are melodramatic and declamatory to an extreme, but consistent with Frías' aim to popularize Mexican history and to awaken sentiments of patriotism, particularly among the masses.

The *Biblioteca del niño mexicano* relates historical events taken from preconquest times through the North American intervention in five chronologically ordered series. Directed to an imaginary group of youthful listeners, the stories make frequent calls to "my little friends," as Frías spins an aura of suspense and mystery: "How deep and forbidding is the night! The old banana fields shudder, shaken by the north winds. . . . Such sadness, my little friends! . . .

It is the night of horror"![10]

These narratives also share the intense and emotional patriotism, the compassion for the Indians, and the admiration for the Mexican people already seen in the *Leyendas históricas* and *Episodios militares*. But here one finds no veiled commentary on present times, except to render lip service to Díaz, the *Caudillo:* "Mexico was starting life; it was a child-nation! . . . What errors, failures, sorrows, and disappointments it was to suffer! . . . Many years still remained before the men who were to give it security, riches, and well-being would come.

The man who was to offer it the most precious gift—peace—was not yet even born! . . ."[11]

D   In Praise of Porfirio Díaz

Frías' homage to the dictator is most blatant in this small booklet of thirty pages, entitled *El General Félix Díaz* and written in 1901, on the thirtieth anniversary of the death of Félix Díaz, the president's brother. In 1871, Félix had formed an army in Oaxaca to support Porfirio's first unsuccessful revolt. In the short but savage guerilla war that followed, Félix was captured, tortured, and murdered, while Porfirio, the future president, escaped only by taking refuge in the mountains of Nayarit.[12]

Frías was commissioned to write this booklet in memory of Félix Díaz by Antenor Sala, editor of *El Progreso Industrial*, to whom Frías directs a letter of thanks in his prologue. Also accompanying *El*

General Félix Díaz are a portrait of the general and an introduction by Frías' close friend José Ferrel.[13] In terms of content, *El General Félix Díaz* offers little real information about its subject. This may be because the story of Félix Díaz was so well known and so oft-repeated at that time, but it is also likely that the booklet was penned in haste and without the benefit of research. Whatever the cause, the work's resemblance to an after dinner speech, or rather an extended toast to an inebriated guest, is striking: "Trace his silhouette? . . . Determine his profile? . . . Narrate his history? . . . Lament his death? . . . No! . . . Because he is one of those who do not need it" (p. 10).

This said, Frías restates the salient episodes of Félix Díaz' life from 1855, when he and his brother rebeled against Santa Anna, to his death by torture in 1871. Indulging for the most part in laudatory passages like the one cited above, Frías provides little concrete information. Battles and campaigns are merely mentioned, in sharp contrast to other military commentaries, in which Frías records events with a quartermaster's eye for detail. Some emphasis is placed on Díaz' personality. Frías takes care to depict him as a warlike and impetuous man, fiercely loyal to his friends and implacable to his enemies. Above all, he is a simple man:

> But Félix Díaz could not be a strategist. . . . his proud character, . . . his dauntless steadfastness, made him better fit for cavalry—in exploration, guerrilla warfare, or cargo.
> His brother Porfirio must have understood that, and that is how he used him, so they both rendered immense services to each other. (P. 19)

The real object of the flattery is not difficult to find. Porfirio Díaz stands always in the near background as a guiding and directing force for the impetuous Félix, and as a figure destined for greatness:

> At the end of that three year war we see Félix outdo himself in serving his brother Porfirio, who was beginning to give growth to his splendid wings; the simple man understood, naturally, the profound man of great destiny. (P. 16)

> . . . and what is still noteworthy is the steadfastness of don Porfirio Díaz, since he, lacking in both human and material resources . . . managed to fight! (P. 24)

Terrible times of desolation and darkness that were to bring the present dawn of Peace! (P. 26)

It is apparent, then, that this booklet about Félix Díaz was intended for the eyes of his brother, the president. It is painful to record that in this period of his life, Frías stooped to groveling for favors from the stiff and unyielding tyrant; just seven months before, he had written a similarly flattering prologue for his *Episodios militares mexicanos*. That was in October 1900, and in that same year he praised Díaz in his *Biblioteca del niño mexicano*. At the same time he was trying to wheedle Justo Sierra's Ministry of Education, a haven of sinecures for writers, into granting him a post, and not long after would even seek refuge in Díaz' army. But to no avail. Humiliating as it was for Frías to bend his knee to the dictatorship for a time, he was never forgiven, and when his fortunes changed, he at least returned to the oppositionist camp with a clear voice and a clean record.

E The Life of Juan the Soldier

Written in better times, and free from every tinge of servility, *La vida de Juan Soldado (The Life of Juan the Soldier)* was published in 1918 by the Imprenta Franco-Mexicana.[14] Free also from the romantic grandiloquence found in the earlier historical works, this booklet of eighteen pages is written in realistic and unpretentious language. The title page announces it as part of an unpublished book, "Heroismos mexicanos" ("Mexican Heroism"), and so we are left with another tantalizing fragment of Frías' many unpublished, and now lost, works. This interesting and highly readable booklet is actually a prosification of popular ballads of the past century concerning a mythical soldier, Juan Soldado, who fought and died in the Three Years' War.[15] Frías explains that he collected the story from *corridos*, or popular narrative ballads, heard at fairs and circuses, at "brawls and shotgun weddings," and that he was thus able to piece together the story presented in this brief work.

However, Frías does more than just that. He makes Juan a symbol of the Mexican soldier, the ragged conscript who periodically fights Mexico's wars. Frías' description of the typical foot soldier of the day is a fine word portrait reminiscent of the more than real caricatures of Guadalupe Posada:[16] ". . . a drawn-out lump of blackish flesh more or less wrapped in tatters of cotton, khaki, pepper-

and-salt, or coarse blue cloth; shod, when not barefoot, with sandals or enormous boots; crowned by a ridiculous headdress, stiff and awkward, called a *chaco*, all of which was attached to a rifle, saber, or lance. That object was a bit more than monkey and something less than free Indian . . . (p. 40).

The story of Juan Soldado, as Frías tells it, begins with his conscription into the federal forces. He learns the trade of soldiery by dint of kicks and curses, but he learns well and is soon respected by his comrades. He also learns the fear and glory of battle. Then he deserts and becomes a bandit, later enlisting in the services of Benito Juárez. He falls in love and becomes briefly lyrical, in a rough-hewn fashion:

> How cute, how pretty,
> Is my latest "little lady";
> The smooth guys
> Can't take her from me!
> Woe to the sergeant
> Who tries to bed her!
> Even don Benito
> Would try to get her;
> She's my rose, little rose
> Of orange-blossom and cinnamon! (P. 15)

Finally, Juan dies for having shot a sergeant who molested his "little lady." Frías notes, however, that he left a son, the Juan Soldado of the French intervention, and that perhaps there will be a day "when, after Juan Soldado, the volunteer of the horrendous revolution, there will come a Juan who will till his own field, who will know how to read, who will not die for the *caudillos*, but will instead live for his family and his country. . . ."(p. 18)[17]

F   Popular Historical Album of Mexico City

Frías' wish for Juan Soldado seemed to be on the threshold of fulfillment in 1925 when he co-authored with Rafael Martínez this popularized history of Mexico City, written, as the introduction states, for "worker-citizens."[18] Frías and Martínez dedicated the attractively illustrated volume to "Juan Soldado," along with Quetzalcóatl, Bartolomé de las Casas, Fernández de Lizardi, and a host of other figures who "worked, struggled, and died for love of the humble working classes of the Valley of Mexico" (dedicatory page). It ostensibly appeared as a commemorative souvenir of the city's six hundredth year celebration, in May 1925, of the founding of Tenochtitlán, and the extreme rarity of the volume indicates that it had a very small printing and a selective distribution.[19]

The *Album*'s purpose coincides with postrevolutionary Mexico's stated aim of popularizing knowledge and the arts and of raising the working and peasant masses' patriotic vision of Mexico's culture and heritage. Such had been Frías' aim throughout his career, and the *Album* clearly reflects Frías' patriotic verve, in spite of some lengthy and lofty quotations from the histories of Clavijero, Alamán, Orozco y Berra, Niceto de Zamacois, and others.[20]

The *Album*'s episodic history traces Mexico City from its founding as Tenochtitlán in the fourteenth century to the presidency of Plutarco Elías Calles. The tone of the work shows clearly that the authors considered that Mexico's travails were coming to an end and that a new day was dawning. They emphasize the masses' suffering throughout past centuries and conclude by noting a fundamental change in the "common soul of the Metropolis": "It is no longer sad, hypocritical, and blustering. Today it works and enjoys, clothes itself and puts on shoes, sings and dances, drinks less *pulque*, throws off the grubby shawl, the fetid sandal, and the lice-ridden sarape of the "down and outs" of the Colonial, Iturbidist, Santannist, and Porfirian Ages" (final page, unnumbered).

The leftist tendencies of the day, to which Frías and Martínez subscribed, give rise to a number of curiosities sprinkled here and there in the text: Jesus Christ is described as a revolutionary, Quetzalcóatl and Las Casas are termed socialists, and Fernández de Lizardi "sided with the proletariat." With obvious significance, the book's appearance, and the ceremony it commemorated, are dated May 1, the communist world's May Day, and the final pages are adorned with strong-armed, square-jawed—and European-looking—youths bearing rifles and sledgehammers.

Given Frías' sympathy for the masses and his aversion for Mexico's recent dictatorship, it is not surprising that he fell into the spirit of the day and embraced Mexico's Marxist fervor. In speaking of the Díaz dictatorship, the two authors exude a certain self-satisfied "we were there" when they describe "the frightful Belén Jail, where we, the first Anti-Caesarian journalists and workers, were tortured" (fourth page, unnumbered). Whether Frías could have continued marching to that rhythm, or whether he would have rebeled at the direction that Mexico later took, is futile to discuss. The fact is that a scant six months after the publication of the *Album histórico*, the controversial author of *Tomochic* was dead.

II Contemporary Satire and Short Stories

A The Pirates of the Boulevard

"[A] Parade of Social and Political Parasites and Snakes in Mexico" is Frías' provocative subtitle for this book, published by Botas in 1915.[21] Originally, the sketches that comprise it were written for the newspaper *El Constitucional* in 1910. As the title suggests, we are brought before a gallery of social types to be found in Mexico's capital in the waning years of the Díaz dictatorship. This was the "Paris-Tenochtitlán" from which Frías took much of his material. Of the forty-two articles in the published collection, the majority depict those whom Frías calls the "peacocks," the ostentatious rich, the effeminate dandies, and the gaudy women that could be seen riding in carriages or early motorcars or parading along the boulevard: men strutting about with bright blazers and diamond-studded walking sticks, women ablaze in feather, bustle, and parasol. Rich or not, they are painted in these stories with a malicious blend of accuracy and caricature, as a pageant of gossips, hypocrites, troublemakers, swindlers, adulterers, homosexuals, and prostitutes.

In these sketches, as in *Tomochic*, *¿Aguila o sol?*, and elsewhere, Frías unleashes his talent for caricature, and his word portraits—unexcelled in all of Latin American literature—become ferocious as he creates mocking and grotesque verbal etchings:

> He is a cherub. His face is truly angelic; pure, fresh, rosy, exquisitely framed by a necklace of silky blond beard, short and curled. . . . Set this seraphic little head onto a curved body, quick and slender, dressed irreproachably in the style of an authentic gentleman, a legitimate one, as if this "doll" had been spirited away from a crowded square in London; a long double-breasted waistcoat snugly fitted to a graceful waistline, light-colored trousers with a Brittanically austere cut, and in his delicately gloved left hand, the glove of his right hand which, bared with provocative coquetry, grasps his rich walking cane of gold, ebony, and ivory. (Pp. 20–21)

Is she old?
Far better if she were. [. . .] Imagine an ashen face, covered with a thick reddish fuzz . . . a fuzz that forms sideburns and a real moustache . . . thick eyebrows that give terrible ferocity to her sunken, feverish eyes. . . . Deep wrinkles on her forehead and on her dry cheeks testify to old age, but her erect torso, vigorous, flexible and shapely, reveals a woman conquered, but not by age. (P. 13)

His run-of-the-mill and perfectly commonplace conversation passed unnoticed by me; I heard only the feminine timber of his voice, while his perfume sickened me; I saw only his heavy, expressionless eyes and his manner, studiously affected so as to show off even more the exotic glimmer of his jewels and the idiotic majesty of a huge chrysanthemum, laughing in the buttonhole of his pearl gray jacket. (P. 103)

Frías obviously had no love for these "peacocks"; through such descriptions one perceives clearly the extent of his revulsion toward the smug and ostentatious imitators of Paris and London. In effect, the descriptions *are* the stories, for there is little or no plot in them, but rather, detailed portraits of people and lifestyles. Reading the *Piratas* is much like walking through a picture gallery of brilliant, grotesque, disturbing caricatures: Goyas, Nasts, Brueghels, and Beerbohms.

Distrust of city life, always a strong current in Frías' writings, is never far from the surface as Frías paints his swindlers, adulterers, and other forms of urban low-life. His attention and his sympathy are extended more than occasionally to a recurring character, the honest and wholesome country person who comes to Mexico City only to contract its infectious corruption. Speaking of this type in general, Frías (who doubtless remembered his own situation as a youth) wrote that "in our capital, the 'slickers' who surround and stalk the luckless 'hicks' . . . are capable of twisting the most practical horsetrader into a good-for-nothing, all puffed up with overbearing 'foreignism' " (p. 58).

In the same vein, Frías' aversion to Modernism in literature is reaffirmed in *Los piratas del boulevard.* He speaks caustically of the "latest nightmarish patriotic ode of José Juan Tablada" and of "the most abominable rhymed toast of Don Juan Didapp or any other long-haired Modernist of the secretariat of public instruction, in Justo Sierra's time" (p. 60). Speaking of Modernism as a social cancer of the likes of opium or gonorrhea, Frías censures its "gilded absurdities" and "dangerous illusions," which prevent young people from learning of life as it truly is and so brings them to temptation (p. 72). Nor does his aversion confine itself to the Modernists' work; on the contrary, it embraces their dissolute way of life, their hedonistic habits and affected Victorian naughtiness, and perhaps more than anything else, their success, for at times the palate senses in Frías the tang of sour grapes. After all, he attempted—and failed—to win an appointment in Sierra's secretariat of public instruction.

In any case, to Frías, the verses of Darío and Gutiérrez Nájera clearly were inseparable from the wanton life of the perfumed, monacled frequenters of the Jockey Club and other stylish gathering places, and in his eyes the effects of such decadence were terrible to behold, as exemplified by the innocent young girl who took up company in this high life until "Modernism took her . . . oh misfortune . . . and ruined her! Style, the epidemic of style, injected it into her . . . and she too, the girl from Guadalajara—who would have guessed it—became a Modernist!" (p. 99). This finger-shaking, moralizing attitude is the dominant note in *Los piratas*, as one after another Frías attacks those vices that he has seen in Mexico City. We can see that this sermonizing tendency runs strong in all his works and connects him firmly to the tradition of José Joaquín Fernández de Lizardi.

There is also a possibility that these vitriolic vignettes were directed at known individuals in the capital city, for the descriptions, detailed as they are, must surely have had models, considering that caricatures and satirical articles alluding to actual personages were common in the newspapers of the day. Frías' own words may be taken as a confession that his articles were similarly conceived when in *Los piratas del boulevard* he writes that "one must, then, read between the lines. The inner circle, the editing staff, and even the court of the victims all know the key, decipher voluptuously, the victims laugh—and all, even the victims, applaud the witty chronicler" (p. 96).

B   The Short Stories

Not all of Frías' shorter works, however, were of the biting and caustic sort that make up *Los piratas del boulevard*. When he turned his attention from the "peacocks," he often wrote of the "doves" and "sparrows" of the less fortunate classes or, as was often the case, of himself. In doing so, he mellowed his tone to one of gentle irony or even of sentimentality. Under the headings of "Historias vivas" ("Living Stories"), "Realidades de la cárcel" ("Realities of the Jail"), "Realidades del pueblo" ("Realities of the People"), "Miserias de México" ("Miseries of Mexico"), and "Cáscaras y semillas" ("Peelings and Seeds"),[22] Frías scattered among the newspaper-reading public a panoply of articles about the working class and the poor, with an outlook of melancholy and sympathy. These stories center around unhappy lives, family tragedies, wasted hopes, and innocent souls brought to grief.

Notably lacking in these stories, if they may be compared to *Los piratas del boulevard,* is the outraged puritanism found in the latter. A reader who had become accustomed to his better known satirical works finds all the more surprising the story of a poor and simple prostitute and her reaction when, having recieved a false jewel from a client, she cheerfully shrugs off her loss, saying: "I lost, aunty, he tricked me, but . . . you only learn by losing!"[23] More surprising still are the pathos of a comely young clerk who toils, year after year, in a clothing store to support her aged parents,[24] or the misfortune of a man who inherits a haunted *chinampa.*[25] Unable to sell his new property, he resolves to live there with his family. Repeated offerings to the Virgin Mary are of no avail as he loses his children one by one and finally drowns.

As in *Los piratas del boulevard,* story line, if present, is usually slight and subservient to description, making clear once again that Frías' eye was as sharp in still life and portraiture as in action scenes:

And Teresa, after three months in Mexico City, already combed her hair splendidly, with nearly Japanese grace, and placed a fine broad ribbon over her black locks with a flirting air, while over firm shoulders a shawl swayed gaily to the breathing rhythm of a bosom that peered firm and round from under the percale of her blouse.[26]

The old man with his creole look of a warlike patriarch—the old corsair with his huge, drooping mustache, his dry, wrinkled face in a collar of ashen beard, his bushy eyebrows and wild eyes. . . .[27]

The little old ladies have beady, weepy eyes, hollowed cheeks, twisted noses, and mouths that sink toothless into strange grimaces, showing off the ugliness of their faces and their bristly, but pleasant, chin whiskers.[28]

These are exerpts of brief, sure portraits, drawn with sympathetic realism and an outstanding talent for choosing a few characteristics rather than resorting to full descriptions. However, even his love for the downtrodden cannot fully keep in rein his penchant to caricature; the following is a grotesque picture in the tragicomic vein of a Chaplin: "His own companions of the pedagogical battlefields called him 'the walking overcoat.' And so he was. You should have seen the astonishment of passers-by as they spied that runtish creature, wrapped from neck to toe in an oversized black overcoat with a drawn out tail that was towed along by his scrawny legs, bowed like those of an outlandish dwarf."[29]

Like *Los piratas del boulevard,* many of these stories are rich in social commentary. His low opinion of the wealthy and comfortable bourgeoisie, as evident in these stories as elsewhere, shows itself as scathing irony in a story (not far removed from the style of *Los piratas del boulevard*) in which a rich father, who has condoned, even encouraged, all manner of outrages of his degraded sons, dies of grief and shame when his daughter marries a hard-working but, alas, poor young man.[30] Although the lengthy sermons found in his novels are missing here, Frías seldom allows the reader to forget where his true sympathies lie.

A small number of Frías' stories, not originally intended for newspapers but rather for literary journals, are altogether different in theme and style. In them Frías departed from brief descriptive sketches and embarked upon fuller development of plots and characters. These are true short stories. Two of his finest are "El almuerzo" ("The Breakfast") and "Los perros de Tomochic" ("The Dogs of Tomochic").[31] The first is a touching breakfast scene between a young officer on barracks duty and his girlfriend. Although slightly marred by an overly long introduction, the story unfolds entertainingly as the two lovers indulge in the bittersweet flirtations and frustrations of a budding romance. In doing so they reveal two souls wounded by past tragedies, each of whom is seeking trust and solace in the other. In the second story the Tomochic tragedy again surfaces, this time through the eyes of an unlettered soldier. Here he tells of the smoldering remains of the village, where now dogs howl over their dead masters' bodies and fight with bands of hungry pigs. This is a macabre scene, masterfully told, as it evokes in jarring contrast the dark vastness of the surrounding mountains and the brutish drama that unfolds in the valley below amidst howling and grunting animals.[32]

These two stories show what Frías was capable of achieving when his talents were used to the fullest. "Los perros de Tomochic" is truly impressive in its force of description. It is a phantasmagoric dirge in a violent, nightmarish minor key. "El almuerzo," on the other hand, is Frías' tour de force of sensitive, artful character development. It is no coincidence, surely, that these excellent stories share with Frías' best novels the fact that they are autobiographical—or so we may judge, since Frías' alias, Miguel Mercado, figures in both.

C Poetry and Drama

Our author often spoke of himself as a "wretched poetaster" or a "miserable versifier," and as a young man he apparently wrote a considerable amount of poetry, for which he gained a certain neighborhood fame. As a schoolboy he wrote a poem against the government, which caused disciplinary action to be brought against him; later, a poem composed about Justo Sierra haunted him in leaner days, like a scarlet letter sewed to his breast, when he sought to obtain a position in the ministry of public education. Among his friends he was known for improvising amusing verses, particularly when he and his circle of admirers were well provisioned with alcohol.

Clearly, these were not the sort of poems likely to be published, and they have long ago disappeared. Frías' published poetry in newspapers and literary reviews is of a vastly different sort, centering around love, jealousy, and, not surprisingly, the hardships of the soldier. Following are two of Frías' poems which were published in the prestigious *El Mundo Ilustrado* of 1896:

Your Kiss[33]

> How white you come to the forges' heat
> Where crusted irons thunder
> Down to the hidden hell where beat
> The plaints of my soul's own hunger.
> Down to my misery, down you are flown
> You see all the pains that corrode
> At the soul that adores you; pains that adorn
> The lines of this sad, sad ode.

And you kiss me in pity . . . and shine, and glow
In Erebus a tunic of light.
With brilliance Olympic, a moment's flow
As compassion's kiss you bring bright;
A star to the brain's obscurist hall
Under the black dome of my skull.

Sinner in Dreams[34]

Deep is the shadow and long is the gloom
That floats, softly torn by the light;
A golden broach of lamp illumes
Naught but the curtains. 'Tis night.

The smiling virgin's face lies framed
By the pillow, and bathed in the flow
Of nocturnal peace, her fragile sleep
Haloed by curls' golden glow.

Now suddenly tense, with her head on her arm
This beauteous one sees with a sigh,
In the depths of the world that lies locked in her mind,
A scene of romance passing by.

A man of her dreams, whom she has not seen
In her life, with a voice that brings bliss,
Swears passionate love . . . and before Christ above
And the Cross in her room, they kiss.

The damsel awakes, and in fevered alarm
Bolts up from her snow-white sheets;
Pale in the tenuous shadows and gloom
With shame unconsoled, she weeps.

"Forgive me," she cries, "for I have sinned!"
"Lord, that man, I never have seen!"
And long in the night, she gives voice to her plight:
The virgin who prays at the altar of Him
Who true crimes of passion forgives!

"Your Kiss" is a sonnet of psychopathological overtones that recalls the verses of the Columbian José Asunción Silva, but lacks the inner rhythms of the latter. The romantic anguish and the subject of the poem suggest that here, as elsewhere, Frías is strongly inclined toward Romanticism, but the reference to Erebus[35] and the "brilliance Olympic" hint that Frías was partially swayed by his Modernist contemporaries in spite of his public scorn for them. The

Other Works of Frías

poem's ending is a jolting one, with its reference to the skull's "black dome," yet it harks back to Espronceda's hair-raising allusions, made at the height of Spanish Romanticism. "Sinner in Dreams" develops once again the theme of guilt in one of the few strokes of religious piety that appear in Frías' secular and often anticlerical writings. The innocence of the young girl who prays forgiveness for an imagined sin is touching, particularly as we are reminded that Frías' life was of the worldly sort to which he refers in the final line. Some nodding acknowledgment of the Modernists is seen here, too, as Frías utilized the fourteen syllable alexandrine line, a late medieval verse form resuscitated by Rubén Darío and brought into some degree of popularity by his Modernist followers.

Frías, an admirer of Naturalism, essayed that form of literary expression most clearly in another poem, "Sara."[36] Accompanied by an article by Rubén M. Campos that lauded the triumph of Naturalism and termed Frías a profound writer in spite of his youth (he was then twenty-five), the poem expounded the tragedy of an innocent young man brought to grief by a prostitute, Sara. In three parts (441 lines), this variation of Emile Zola's *Nana* relates the pious youth's seduction and his ultimate degradation and death from "a horrible infirmity." There are many passages reminiscent of Zola's naturalistic novels in which sickness, vice, and squalor are dwelled upon in graphic terms; nevertheless the poem, with its long and agonized emphasis on temptation and remorse and its exaggerated emotions, underscores once again Frías' essentially Romantic approach to literature. Furthermore, the hero dies in true Spanish Romantic fashion: delirious and with a priest at his side, while in the background wind and lightning lash the night. In his poetry, as elsewhere, Frías' approach to literature was paved with bombast and emphasis, not subtlety; much of his verse thumps along uncadenced and dissonant, but its very strength derives from emotion, viril and unfettered. Essentially a barroom poet by inclination, he might have penned epic and heroic verses if his times had given him epic material instead of a static and musclebound dictatorship. Indeed, his poems have an unmistakable epic flair when he gives poetic vent to his twin loves of heroic war and patriotism. "Asalto" ("Assault") has its moments of rough martial splendor:

> . . . The drum is pounding thunderously,
> The furious trumpet sounds attack
> A thousand sparks of light appear

>   as weapons glisten in the sun
>   foretelling of the slaughter near. . . .[37]

But such successes are rare and brief. Remembering that Cervantes too was a failed poet could have been little comfort to Frías, who never gave up writing poems though he published none in his later years. This unpublished sonnet, likely from the years 1920–1925, captures Frías' epic spirit but happily avoids the excessive fanfare and bombast found in his earlier verses.

> At last fierce Hamlet has regained his mind,
> For now he dreams and vacillates no more.
> His books are closed, the specter's fear is o'er
> To weeping Ophelia he declares, "I want
> To be, to be, to conquer! If I die
> The greatest peace of all I'll wrest from war.
> Come out from the convent. Wait in the fields."
> She answers with joy, "I'll wait for you here."
> To be or not to be? Out with the sword:
> 'Tis time for swiftness of action borne of faith,
> Above the life that blood covers over as gold,
> In victory as only the victory sacred can be.
> And while he fights in the night til the dawn,
> She awaits in the fresh-plowed field, and sings.[38]

Here again, Frías is writing of himself (he often called himself a vacillating "Hamlet"). This is the Frías of later years, the matured Frías found in ¿*Aguila o sol?*, who has conquered himself, who willingly takes on epic struggles against great odds. How different from the melodramatic, self-pitying Frías of earlier writings! Unfortunately, great thoughts do not always result in great poetry, and this poem lacks the cadence and sonority that one expects to hear in a good sonnet.

Frías was not destined for immortality as a poet, but he fared even less well as a dramatist. We know little about his plays. They were not published, and newspapers and accounts of the time say nothing about their performances, so we must depend on Frías' own description of two *género chico* (vaudeville) plays, which were reportedly written in 1906.[39] The Mexican *género chico* consisted of short musical farces, generally loaded with grotesque and crude humor, obscene allusions, and clownish acting. Frías' "Zarzuela" ("Interlude") and "El Caimán" ("The Cayman") were not exceptions: "Zarzuela," Frías recounts, was a parody on the Adam and Eve theme in which Eve was to sing a song entitled "El tango de la manzana" ("The Apple Tango"). Not surprisingly, the work was found objectionable for the stage. "El Caimán" was an underworld farce concerning a pickpocket of that name. Although it reached the boards, it failed resoundingly on the first night. Whether the plays deserved their respective fates is difficult to say, since they are lost; according to Frías' retelling, the demise of "El Caimán" was due to poor acting. This may well have been true, but it is significant that Frías never again took the plunge into drama.

The unfortunate results of Frías' attempts at "pure" literature and at literature for entertainment dramatize his inescapable marriage to the social realities of Mexico, for when he tried to divorce himself from these realities both technique and inspiration failed him. He clearly is at his best when seeking out the soul of the Mexican people. This he does with penetrating clarity, writing with confidence and feeling—if not always with great finesse—and above all, with vigor. In this respect, Frías was most surely out of phase with his epoch, for literature during the *Porfiriato* was dominated by escapism and warmed over European stylishness. Given the spirit of the times, it was clearly too much to expect either literary critics or the learned reading public to respond to the likes of Heriberto Frías.

CHAPTER 5

Some Observations: Four Keys to Frías

I *The Novel of the Mexican Revolution*

IF a direct line could be drawn between Fernández de Lizardi, Mexican novelist of the times of independence, and Mariano Azuela, novelist of the Mexican revolution, that line would surely intersect the work of Heriberto Frías.[1] As interpreters of their surroundings, their jaundiced and penetrating views provide sure portraits of their respective historic moments. If we join Wellek and Warren in the view that the novel traces its evolution to the chronicle, these writers are, in the world of novelists, mutants and throwbacks in a chain of expressive evolution.[1] Their works contain much of that modern chronicle, the newspaper, as they narrate, describe, and editorialize. In them, finesse of style and structure are frankly secondary to linear narration and the force of emphasis. Their line is a robust one, including not only Fernández de Lizardi, Frías, and Azuela, but also such other Mexican writers as Manuel Payno, Luis G. Inclán, José Tomás de Cuéllar, Gregorio López y Fuentes, José Mancisidor, Mauricio Magdaleno, Jorge Ferretís, and Luis Spota. Engrossing storytellers at their best, pedantic drum-thumpers at their worst, some of their works are novels only because they and Mexican literati choose generously to classify them as such. Virtually all modern Mexican prose literature is variously enriched and tainted by their influence. Most significantly, their current has converged in this century with the stream of history, and out of Mexico's decade of turmoil emerged the Novel of the Mexican Revolution.

Defining the Novel of the Mexican Revolution has proved to be a difficult task and one yet to be done to everyone's satisfaction; nevertheless, the wave of novels associated in this group tend to have certain like characteristics. Primarily attempts to depict and interpret the revolution, these novels are usually memoirs or semimemoirs; thus they offer a subjective and necessarily partial viewpoint of then recent events. They are told in a variety of styles, but are generally simple, episodic, realistic, and oriented to the journalistic approach. Many novels follow the Marxist-flavored view of the revolution by focusing on the masses' role in that event, but actual political viewpoints vary from prorevolutionary (Mancisidor) to openly sceptical (Azuela). The cycle begins with Azuela's *Los de abajo* (*The Underdogs*), published in 1915, and ends with Agustín Yáñez' *Al filo del agua* (*The Edge of the Storm*) of 1947. In actual practice, all novels of this cycle inevitably are compared to *Los de abajo* as the archetype and essence of its kind.[3]

Tomochic's recounting of massed and armed revolt against the Díaz regime foresees much of what later came to embody the Novel of the Revolution. Except for *Tomochic*, the idea of mass uprising is strangely absent in prerevolutionary Mexican literature, even though such events occurred often during the early 1890s; but as early as the first edition of 1893, Frías captures the rumblings of *potential* mass action in his picture of proud villagers unwilling to bow before the dictator's whip, who take up arms to defend their freedom, their love of land, and their way of life. Inasmuch as both *Tomochic* and *¿Aguila o sol?* concentrate on the Mexican countryside, where the revolution was ultimately to take shape, they both foresee the archetype of the Novel of the Revolution's typically rural setting. Both of these novels center upon the despotism and the cruelty that Díaz inflicted upon the rural masses during his regime and show pointedly that somehow the downtrodden might spring back. *¿Aguila o sol?* shows provincial Mexico symbolized in "Mixtlán," with its fourteen churches and a single schoolhouse, its ruling family and the "brutish political boss," but above all, it lays bare a neomedieval imbalance of property, power, and human rights, all of which ultimately led to rebellion. *¿Aguila o sol?* has this important point of contact with Yáñez' *Al filo del agua*, as they both show Mexico on the brink of revolt during the electric moments of stillness that come before the storm.

But these are external factors. More importantly, Frías moved ahead of his time stylistically and opened the door, not only to the Novel of the Mexican Revolution, but also to the twentieth century

Realistic novel. *Tomochic's* episodic chapters (which surely seemed jumpy and jerky to nineteenth century readers accustomed to abundant detail and smooth transitions) are forerunners of Azuela's collagelike narrative. Its spare, lean framework, overspread by direct and suggestive descriptions held together by dialogue (in later editions beginning with that of 1906), are also strongly connected. Most particularly, Frías' earthy characterizations of Mexican soldiers and rural types have led R. Anthony Castagnaro to claim that many passages could be taken from *Tomochic* and inserted into any of various Novels of the Revolution "and seem a natural part of their literary habitat." Castagnaro further declares that *Tomochic* is perhaps the first instance in Mexican novelistic history that "characters are captured with such essential verisimilitude that they can be nothing but Mexican."[4]

Historians of Mexican literature generally agree that *Tomochic* anticipates the Novel of the Revolution. One by one, beginning with Beals' affirmation that "Azuela . . . consciously or unconsciously borrows from his predecessor, Heriberto Frías," through Castagnaro's recent declaration that *Tomochic* is the "most important" of the cycle's precursors, there is no disagreement on this matter.[5] Still, *Tomochic's* relative obscurity remains, in spite of its historical importance as well as its considerable literary merits.

Mariàno Azuela reflects in *Cien años de novela mexicana* that he first heard of *Tomochic* from the American critic and Mexicanist Carlton Beals, when Beals claimed that Azuela had plagiarized *Tomochic* in writing *Los de abajo*. His curiosity piqued "to get to know the novel that I plagiarized," Azuela read *Tomochic* and declared it among "the most authentically national" of Mexican novels and expressed pride in having been connected with Frías' early work.[6]

Frías' last novel, with which he deliberately set out to write his trilogy of the revolution, is less widely recognized for its place in that movement. In fact, many critics speak knowledgeably of *Tomochic* but appear not even to have read *¿Aguila o sol?*. If Frías had lived to complete his trilogy, it might have been one of the most memorable of the Novels of the Revolution, since Frías' own life during those years makes it abudantly clear that he had much to say. Like other novels of this cycle, *¿Aguila o sol?* was written in retrospect as an attempt to sort out the causes and meanings of the recent holocaust. It shows Mercado's evolution from an aimless and defeated oppositionist to a revolutionary with a new purpose in his political life. At the time of its writing, revolutionary ardor in Mexico was at its peak, and ¿*Aguila o sol?* represents a clear break, ideologically, from *Tomochic*, in which he insisted that armed rebellion, however heroic it may be, could only end in the disaster of Mexican killing Mexican. Notwithstanding Frías' change of political stance, ¿*Aguila o sol?* maintains the same pre-Azuelan directness of style and heady Mexican flavor—considered apt for a barroom raconteur but wholly unfit for literary purposes—that gave *Tomochic* its refreshing unpretentiousness. Azuela's *Los de abajo* was not "discovered" until 1925, whereupon the literary fad did an abrupt about face; meanwhile both Azuela and Frías wrote as outcasts in a literary vacuum.

Thus the very soul of Frías' writing sets him sharply apart from the more celebrated Mexican authors of his time, such as Gamboa, López-Portillo, Delgado, Gutiérrez Nájera, and others who were forgers of careful and self-conscious works of artistry, meant to be read by the lettered elite. Frías (and later writers who followed Azuela) spoke to the masses without artistic pretense, trusting to vigor, truth, and undeniable *mexicanidad* for impact. Frías serves as the bridge between Lizardi, Inclán, Cuéllar, and Rabasa, who were frankly nineteenth century writers of this tendency, and the Azuela "school" of this century. Frías' connection with these writers lies also in his concern with the middle class, which he hopes to awaken into self-reform. His is a tragic sense of dealing with middle class vulgarities; lacking the burlesque sense of humor that characterizes the nineteenth century writers of this group, Frías' dark and brooding *Tomochic* and sardonic ¿*Aguila o sol?* place him in closer proximity to the writers of 1920–1940. If strict categorizations be demanded, *Tomochic* should be placed as precursor to the Novel of the Revolution, and ¿*Aguila o sol?* should be given its deserved ranking wholly within that grouping.

Frías' influence on later writers is, however, doubtful. His last novel was published, and he lay dead, before Azuela's novels began to receive public acclaim. Thereafter, all eyes looked to Azuela as the leader in this new national literature. Occasional critics, among them Francisco Monterde, René Avilés, and Ernest R. Moore, have remembered Frías and lamented his obscurity, but no evidence exists to hint that he altered the flow of Mexican literature by influencing younger writers. Rather, his place is that of a vertebra in a strong spine of likeminded Mexican authors who shared his earthy tendencies, and his particular value lies in his having written boldly and honestly during exceedingly difficult times.

II *Positivism*

In an era dominated by the careful literary craftsmanship of such writers as Gamboa, López-Portillo y Rojas, and Gutiérrez Nájera, the works of Frías stand out like plumber's tools on a banquet table. Sacrificing style for sincerity and artistry for indignation, Frías struggled to interpret Mexican life as he saw it and lived it.

As a man in and of the middle class, though, unable to accept much of what that meant in Porfirian society, Frías saw all too clearly how pecking order and injustice descended from rich to poor. Not knowing the upper classes well enough to do more than heap vague diatribe upon such famous names as Díaz, Limantour, and Sierra, it was natural that the substance of Frías' criticism be directed toward his own—Mercado's—middle class, where his knowledge was most intimate and profound. The major characters of his novels and short stories are staunch bourgeois figures. Even the rustic Julia stands apart from the *Tomochitecos*, having experienced a "parenthesis of cultured life" in earlier days.[7] Frías' spokesman Argüelles says in *El amor de las sirenas* that "we are the Mexican middle class . . . neither good nor bad, but . . . capable of either" (p. 477).

The Mexico of the Díaz period was a thoroughly complacent and bourgeois-directed Mexico, but Frías saw mostly its dingy underpinnings, since his years of persecution, jail, poverty, and ostracism kept him on the outskirts of his own social class. Though deeply repelled by what he saw, he nevertheless could not fully reject his own background or the ethos of a society that had so repeatedly mistreated him. As a partial outsider, his was a vantage point (though not a very enviable one) from which to see beyond the complacency and the shallowness of the period, to mistrust its glitter, and to attack its evils as he saw them, but his viewpoint was always from within.

Frías had neither the taste nor the patience for drawn out subtleties. His analytical radius was small. However, he did realize that he had been mistreated and restricted as a soldier, journalist, and author. In a highly personal manner, and with only a faith in common sense, justice, and truth as the basis for his social thought, he at first reacted instinctively to the pressure of the regime and the oppression of the social order. He feared and despised this oppression, but not until his writing of ¿*Aguila o sol?* in the early 1920s did he show a broader view of the widespread inequalities of power and wealth that prevailed under Díaz and that brought on the terrible upheaval in 1910 and ultimately distinguished it from a merely political change of guard. Thus at first Frías reacted to his "circumstances" (taken in the Ortegan sense), and his criticism was directed toward specific wrongdoings and vices as his reformist urges led him; his cure in each case went no further than the removal of the symptom.

Having no firm base of political thought on which to anchor his convictions, Frías went as the tide carried him once the revolution was set in motion. Initially a fiery *maderista,* he came to say in his editorials of 1914 that the *Presidente Apóstol* had been gullible and naïve. He even found himself, only days before the revolution erupted, defending Porfirio Díaz in the face of an apparent *científico* takeover:

"There was a certain discipline and even a certain love for the Supreme Chief. Many loved him, all feared him, and only the *científicos* or **NEOTRAITORS** hated him, behind their masks."[8]

Frías' attitude toward the revolution itself underwent change. Although he opposed dictatorships, he originally feared the anarchy that revolt might bring. Voicing his middle class apprehension in *Tomochic,* he recoiled at the possibility of a widespread revolt, saying "so much useless bloodshed, then, what a national catastrophe to the advantage of the ambitious . . ." (p. 142); and in ¿*Aguila o sol?* he echoed his fear of chaos while pondering the future: "after Díaz, dictator or anarchy. Bulnes prophesies that there will be law, but whose law? Of the dictatorship or of anarchy?" (p. 316).

On the very eve of the revolution, he called out for serenity and deliberation: "We recognize one danger, the danger of impatience, to which restless spirits are so prone; but we deny the right of violence as the road to salvation. Patriotism counsels us to persist in the true democratic attitude that respects peace and order as bases of all prosperity."[9] Not too long afterwards, however, he appears to be caught up in the spirit of revolt when he writes: "The armed and semiorganized masses scattered throughout the North go slowly, victoriously, threateningly toward the interior, making up a hardened social unit ("Constitutionalist Army"). Flight of the privileged classes. Rejoicing in the middle class that rises up from the bed of its ignominy."[10] Finally, his last published work shows him embracing the Marxist fervor of the decade, calling Jesus Christ a "revolutionary" and Bartolomé de las Casas a "socialist."[11]

Therefore, Frías' political loyalties are, to say the least, mercurial, but this does not mean that his social thoughts are. To explain them, it is necessary to look deeply for the underlying motives in Frías' works, into the personal resentment that he felt and into his longing for a return to constant values and unchanging virtues of life. The injustices that the author suffered during the early years of his life are vividly reflected in the pessimism and bitterness that well up in his works of this period. Novels such as *Tomochic*, *Amor de las sirenas*, *Miserias de México*, and *El triunfo de Sancho Panza*, short stories like "La realidad," and several of his poems wallow in self-pity and pessimism. In others he lashes out in retaliation against those who stand above him in the pecking order; this can be observed in *Los piratas del boulevard* and in his mordant editorials and articles.

El amor de las sirenas is the least condemning of his earlier works, but even it offers little hope for reform. Having dragged themselves through the slime of their acts, the characters of the novel emerge no better or wiser for their experiences; all have descended to the bottom, and no one has managed to rise much, nor do most seem to care. Santiesteban is now a confirmed *debauché*; Lupe has given up as his redeemer, and so turns (impulsively, for she is on an evangelical rebound) to her second choice, Argüelles, who from beginning to end is inert and weak.

By 1910, Frías was writing the articles later published as *Los piratas del boulevard* and composing editorials for *El Constitucional* that make it clear that he is working off his frustration, looking for revenge in his diatribes. In *Los piratas*, the targets for his attacks are invariably the well-to-do bourgeoisie, who flaunt their successes on the streets with gaudy clothes, lovers, cars, and the generally unbridled pursuit of pleasure. Frías' caricatures of the successful, the dishonest, and the degraded members of this class reveal a revulsion that borders on hate. Little wonder, for while being their intellectual and professional equal, he suffered continual poverty, persecution, and humiliation at their hands; as a rebel, he fought them and was consistently defeated; as a moralist, he attempted to awaken them and was completely ignored.

His attitude toward peasants and workers, on the other hand, is one of paternalistic benevolence. Let it be noted that Frías' writings never got very close to the masses; the point of view is one of "them and us," and his really well-drawn characters, as we have noted, are consistently middle class spokesmen. His sympathy and compassion for the lower class' lamentable condition during that period is so great that he will not condemn them, even while criticising their misdeeds. He views them in terms of frailties with much more complacency than he displays in dealing with the perversity or hypocrisy that he sees in the more moneyed classes. In the descriptions of soldiers, *soldaderas*, the masses and their promiscuity, we have the impression that these people have had no choice, as in the common case of servant girls "raped on the straw mat of the kitchen" by the family son and then thrown out to the streets, where prostitution awaits.[12] A kindly priest with whom Miguel Mercado is discussing the problems of the poor, reflects the same opinion regarding their misdeeds and weaknesses: "So they like their jug of *neutle* and their little Lady of Guadalupe? So some get drunk, or many, or all if you please, on holidays? Let us not judge so we may not be judged" (*¿Aguila o sol?* p. 91)

Frías is probably quite correct in implying that the majority of vices among the poor are a result of poverty or ignorance, whereas among the rich these same vices are a mere pasttime. However, in holding the poor blameless, Frías seems also to be saying that they are capable of very little positive action. Even a certain fear of the masses is occasionally seen in Frías' works, sometimes expressed by Miguel Mercado, sometimes by other characters, but always directed toward the anonymous, faceless mass. Says one character, a doctor, in *¿Aguila o sol?*: "They are legion. They are millions of beasts who eat little and produce nothing. If we don't stop that monster, it will do away with us" (p. 86). Of the soldier as a mass, Frías says this: "That object looked like a live, dirty, apparatus of death, a mechanism of murder; a detestable and tragic thing, although ridiculous, that nevertheless was good for toppling governments, sacking evacuated cities, initiating revolts" (*Juan Soldado*, p. 4).

Likewise, the hordes of *soldaderas* cause Miguel Mercado to confess that "he admired and feared them; they inspired in him both tenderness and terror" (*Tomochic*, p. 11); and the same type of reaction is to be observed in his description of the Baratillo district of Mexico City as "an awful hodgepodge of blankets, straw hats and shawls, a stomping about over mud of *pulque* and urine" (*El amor de las sirenas*, p. 440.) The predominantly Indian masses were kept ignorant and helpless by the dictatorship, and Frías quite correctly saw that they were potentially dangerous; it is not surprising that one of his characters should ponder that "the day some scoundrel tells them they can be stronger, that will be . . ." (*¿Aquila o sol?*, p. 86).

Aside from an occasional qualm, however, Frías' main attitude toward the Indians and the masses of the poor is one of fatherly sympathy and compassion. If the revolution occurs, "it will be the punishment for our own sin, for we are to blame," says Padre José Juan to the townspeople of Mixtlán (Ibid.). This good father learned the Indian languages in order to live with them and educate them and in his conversations conveys Frías' hope for the unfortunate lower class. Reflecting an awareness of the very admirable system of rural schools organized by José Vasconcelos during the presidency of Álvaro Obregón (or approximately when this novel, *¿Aguila o sol?*, was being written), the priest organizes secular, practical schools: "He taught them to read. He converted taverns into schools. He showed them how to sell at a good price in large cities the precious colored jars and cups that they patiently modeled and painted like their forefathers" (pp. 38–39).

Still, the great multitudes of the Mexican populace knew only ignorance and humiliation, and in fixing the immediate blame for such a situation, Frías was sure and emphatic: it was the wealthy, the powerful, the corrupt, at whose head stood the dictator Díaz. The regime's iron-fisted policy of *pan o palo* ("bread or beatings") forms the background for most of Frías' novels. In *Tomochic* the army, Díaz' greatest support in maintaining the dictatorship, exterminates a village of fanatical insurrectionists; *Miserias de México* describes another of Díaz' weapons, the adulatory press, with the suppression of journalistic criticism; *¿Aguila o sol?* demonstrates the manner in which the dictatorship controlled a community by supporting the local bosses and then utilizing the army and the political bosses as a whip over the peoples' back. In his newspaper articles,

Frías likewise kept up a lively and belligerent monologue, attacking Díaz, Vice President Corral, and the *científicos,* whom he called, among other things, "Judas, Barrabas, and Company."

In assessing the deeper causes of his country's degraded state, Frías attributed much of the blame to the wealthy, the well-off, and the comfortable of Mexico who were enjoying the fruits of the period's bourgeois prosperity. These groups had the responsibility of creating a solid economic base in a just Mexico, but in Frías' opinion they shunned their responsibility, for he consistently portrays them as being frivolous, gaudy, and depraved. His most grotesque caricatures come from the ostentatious wealthy, such as "Duke Nezahualcóyotl," his crazed wife, and his incestuous children in *El amor de las sirenas.*

At its best, Frías would seem to say, the middle class was an inert mass, grasping servilely at the favors handed down by "Caesar" and his court. The generation of the Díaz period, he laments:

has witnessed and suffered the slow but sure prostitution of the middle class . . . the perversion of the great intellectual mass, save heroic exceptions. The Porfirian dictatorship, sanctioned and supported by the rich, the military, and the clergy, tended systematically to abolish the virility of the middle class, a phenomenon noted in the Federal District, where employees and professionals made up a corrupt palace court that lived in . . . degenerate servility.

In that sad and degenerate social class, which displays or aspires to display a richness that it envies in the so-called aristocracy, there is intellect, and even heart and sentiment, but it lacks the pride and courage to face the intimate struggles of life, much less to confront the tempests of politics.[13]

It must be said that Frías employs a curious double standard when dealing with the separate classes. In general, he is corrosively critical of the well-off, and nothing they do escapes his scorn and indignation. The poorer classes, on the other hand, win Frías' sympathy regardless of their actions. Among this class, the drunkard, the prostitute, or the swindler is portrayed as a poor devil, rather than a doer of misdeeds. Frías surely felt that these classes were simply innocent victims of the social structure, and that their vices and pecadillos were unavoidable because of their ignorance and poverty, while the upper classes sought to cloak their perversity in a chic mantle of respectability. These privileged classes clearly had the means to set an example to the masses as models of virtue, but they failed in this most basic responsibility. This paternalism underscores Frías' adherence to a middle class point of view.

In a like manner, Frías' body of thought, without approaching a constant philosophical system, hovers on the outer edges of Positivism, just as Frías himself is a peripheral bourgeois. He believes strongly in the value of careful research (as shown in his *Episodios militares* and the *Leyendas históricas*, both results of painstaking study) and in the importance of science and material well-being. He likewise shows no interest in religion, except for the material good the church can do or the harm it can bring.

In social matters, Frías reveals himself as a determinist in the best Spencerian Positivist tradition when he implies, as we have noted, that people's motives and actions are influenced by their lot in society. But in insisting that the poor were to be educated, clothed, and fed, our Mexican author could never embrace the unsentimental pseudo-Darwinism that Spencer (and the *científicos*) found so convenient in justifying social imbalances while despising the poor for their poverty and scorning the weak for their weakness. Opposing the Positivist posture, moreover, was Frías' search for honesty and freedom, two items not provided for in the *porfirista* credo and which Frías found difficult to find in the society around him.

As the mature author of *¿Aguila o sol?*, Frías makes explicit both his debt and his opposition to the followers of Gabino Barreda. Gaudelia, Mr. Hanssen, and Miguel Mercado present his final solution and hope for Mexico's future; individually and in chorus, these three voice a plea for order and progress, the reformation of some outmoded institutions (i.e., the idle *charro*, the effete landowner), the injection of new methods of farming and production, peace, and above all, hard work and industry: "Gaudelia, the *mestiza* wife of a new *criollo* Mexican, son of a European immigrant who combined his capital with his work as creator, renovater, and regenerator, would make on the ancestoral land, now well irrigated, happily worked, and justly partitioned, the model home, a cradle of new men" (p. 312).[14]

This particular idea of "new men" brings Frías to the parting of the ways with the most basic Positivist attitude, for the latter preached that science and scientific institutions would bring man to his fullest realization and thus left little need for man to attempt to improve himself. Frías, however, placed more responsibility on the individual, as he continues: "Since neither new institutions, new governments, nor new laws could save the homeland from its enemies from within and without, new men would save it, new men whose bodies would be free from poisons inherited or acquired: alcoholism, syphilis, rapacity, ambition, and hate; their spirits would be free of prejudices and supersititions, both democratic and antidemocratic, both Catholic and anti-Catholic" (Ibid.).

In his insistence upon individual virtues rather than institutional excellence, Frías' morality centers around the avoidance of certain vices (most of which he had experienced) and the cultivation of health, honesty, industry, and a peaceful home life. The following exerpts will typify his thought:

all the social and national ills are rooted in the lack of health; . . . without healthy men there are no worthy citizens. (*Miserias*, p. 18)

I believe in redemption by work, sorrow, and the home. (*El amor de las sirenas*, p. 470)

I have one ideal: sincerity, truth. (*Triunfo*, p. 61)

. . . new blood and new life, discipline and character, schools, books, periodicals, gymnasiums, and new gardens. (*El amor de las sirenas*, p. 477)

If such forthright common sense sounds unsophisticated, it should be remembered that those engaged in an intellectual attack upon Mexican Positivism left even more to be desired. The *Ateneo de la Juventud* ("Atheneum of Youth") was comprised of some thirty-one young Mexican intellectuals who banded together in 1909 and were applauded grandly as they began to take the Positivist credo to task. Yet they never descended from their lofty metaphysical attack to take on the sterner realities of politics, and when the revolution actually came about, only one of their number, José Vasconcelos, even participated in the Maderist movement. "Here then," as John Rutherford puts it, "were many of the brains the Revolution needed, busy discussing the problems of art and philosophy."

Frías was by no means a theorist, and his philosophy, if we may call it that, was of an external and unsubtle sort, but he plumbed the soul of his own period and prescribed what it needed most; for the ignorant and starving masses he saw the need for health and education; for the idlers of all classes he proposed a regimen of honest work; and for a society beset with forced marriages, infidelity, and adultery, Frías advocated a return to the stability of a solid home life. Mexico did not need subtle metaphysics or theologies; what was called for was just the sort of elemental morality upon which Frías insisted in his writings. Without undue theorizing, Frías saw more clearly than the theorists that in his times "the words country, truth, justice, morality, sounded hollow," and that those who were charged with the country's leadership were "converting everything into business, the textbook as well as newspaper, the hospital clinic as well as the university chair" (*Miserias*, p. 49).

But now, having defended Frías for a vision that distinguished the profound from the merely complicated, we must again resist the temptation to call him a seer. It is painfully clear that as political and social events took place, both before and during the revolution, Frías had no better grasp of their broader meaning than anyone else. For example, the Frías of ¿*Aguila o sol?* (if we can take Mercado as an autobiographical mask) is at most a reluctant dragon who delivers his inflaming and revolutionary speech only after considerable doubt and soul searching. Even afterward he is assailed by "painful uncertainty" (p. 296).

The ideals that Frías upheld were closer to reality than the drawingroom rhetoric of the *Ateneo,* but his actual proposals for reform were as amorphous as those of Madero, who died without having formulated a workable plan of social action, or of Azuela, Martín Luis Guzmán, and other writers of the revolution who, even years after the war, were still trying to make sense of the stormy years through which they had passed and who in encounters with *real* revolutionaries saw little more than bandits, gangsters and profiteers. Politically, Frías was molded by events, rather than the reverse, but so too were Azuela, Guzmán, and other writers of the revolution. However, there is one difference, and it is an important one. The clear tendency among the Mexican intellectuals when faced by open warfare was to turn their back ultimately on the revolution in disgust at its ugliness. Caught in the bankruptcy of Madero's free-floating idealism, their disillusionment was complete when in 1914–1916, the issues of the revolution began to be forged out of blood and chaos. However, Frías' experience in Tomochic and his years as an untouchable in the Porfirian caste system had prepared him to look for no quick victories, and political setbacks could not easily lead him into withdrawal or pessimism. It is a mature Frías who in ¿*Aguila o sol?* shows a hesitant Miguel Mercado who freely admits that he has no clear idea of what is going on but maintains his faith in the basic virtues nonetheless and who is willing to speak wryly but goodnaturedly of Mexico's history: ". . . and the revolution began. That was at the morning mass of September 16, 1910, and that war is not over yet, as is only natural, since hardly less than a hundred and ten years have gone by" (p. 277).

III *Naturalism*

By 1890, Mexico's intellectual circles were caught up in the wave of Naturalism, a European ultrarealistic style that was current scientism translated to literature. In effect, Positivism and Naturalism, as both were known and practiced then, were two sides to the same coin. Ideals that placed the material aspect of life over spiritual values, set great store on objective and impartial observation, and in particular evinced faith in social and hereditary determinism were embraced by both. They further displayed Victorian man's unspoken belief that progress held for him an unstoppable march toward the good life if only society were to conform to nature's laws—laws of cause and effect that to the common man boiled down to simplistic and mechanical notions such as "the survival of the fittest" and the idea that heredity plus environment fixed one's lot in life with a certainty theretofore credited only to God, the stars, or fate.

Just as Positivism had been molded over to serve the industrial and financial middle class in its rise to power, Naturalism sought its maximum expression in that essentially middle class literary form, the novel. Led by France's Goncourt brothers and most notably by Emile Zola, the Naturalists took literary Realism down a new path where the scientific attitude sought out and laid bare the invisible strings that pull man, the puppet, to his destiny. Naturalists in Spain (Galdós, Pereda, Pardo Bazán) and in Latin America (Carrasquilla, Gamboa, Acevedo Díaz) were a bit less inclined to deny altogether the spiritual side to life, but they shared wholeheartedly their French *confrères'* reforming urges and their tendency to play up the seamy side of things. Followers, but not purists, the Mexican Naturalists took an especially eclectic view and freely combined

Naturalism, Romanticism, and whatever else they found apt, to the point that the job of classifying authors, never a very fruitful pursuit, becomes an occult art when dealing with Gamboa, Rabasa, López-Portillo y Rojas, Delgado, and, to be sure, Frías. Federico Gamboa is most often held up as Mexico's response to the "scientific novel," but we will see now that Frías was second to no Mexican, even Gamboa, in following the trail of Zola.

There can be no doubt that *Tomochic* takes its inspiration from Zola's great war novel *La Débâcle (The Debacle)*[16] in its plot, style, and characterizations. Without diminishing Frías' own true-to-life story of the Tomochic campaign, his novel (in terms of characterizations, attitudes, and key episodes) is otherwise an adaptation of that French account of the Franco-Prussian War. Apparently both Frías and Zola had much the same message to spell out, so the model was made to order. *La Débâcle* takes pains to expose the frightful mediocrity that eroded the French Army and brought swift, humiliating defeat. Zola presents a dismal picture of ill-trained and undisciplined soldiers, outdated equipment, inept, bumbling officers, and at the top, a clown of monumental dimensions (Napoleon III) who directs the campaign with regal stupidity. We have already seen all this in *Tomochic*. Zola recorded with painstaking accuracy the blunders perpetrated by incompetent leaders, and these, too, find their counterparts in *Tomochic* in the marches and countermarches, the lack of food and rest that weakens soldiers and assures defeat, the evocation of fear and cowardice as green troops first go under fire, and the bitter taste of defeat as officers begin blaming one another to lessen their own disgrace.

Entire scenes from *La Débâcle* crop up in *Tomochic*. The piling of cadavers in the ruins of Tomochic is reminiscent of the heaps of dead in the makeshift hospital at the Hôtel de Ville Delaherche with the same lurid display of limbs, faces, and rotting flesh. Also shared are scenes that show soldiers mad with hunger, who pounce upon anything edible like wild beasts; French troopers who devour a few bits of bread, a stolen slab of meat, a sip of commandeered wine compare with Mexican soldiers who fight over food, brawl over water, and are willing to kill for a hunk of raw meat.

Zola, in whose closely conceived novels *everything* means *something*, used the two young protagonists Maurice Levasseur and Jean Macquart as symbols of two opposing elements in the French Army and in French society at large. Maurice is, in modern parlance, a defective product, a reject. Unbalanced, weak, fickle, and gullible, he finds comfort and support at the side of Jean, who is a solid, simple ex-farmhand whose common sense and uprightness make him a standout around Maurice and his generally loutish barracks-mates. Frías sought a like symbolization of good and bad soldiers and found it. Mercado goes into battle filled with bookish ideas of valor and glory but finds only fear and cowardice in himself during actual combat. Far from making a hero of him, warfare repeatedly brings out his bestial nature, until finally, after the ultimate defeat of the insurgents, he drunkenly mounts a horse and gallops through the battered and burning village shouting "Hurray! . . . Long live death!" (p. 133). Frías' good soldier is Captain Molina, who does everything right; is brave, humane, and cool-headed in battle; and who, like Jean, is something of an exception among his peers. Zola has Maurice killed off to denote the necessity of cutting a rotten limb from a tree (France) so that the healthy branches may survive, but Frías' youthful pessimism causes him to kill Captain Molina instead, leaving a rotting tree (Mexico) with one sound limb less.

Other characters, too, are parallel. Zola's Lieutenant Rochas, a loudmouthed, obscene, and drunken boor, is a faithful prototype of Lieutenant Castorena. Both are fit only for battle, where their rage makes them beautiful: when soldiers begin to bolt in fear, Rochas turns on them with brandished sword, threatening them "to do as you're told, if not, the first man to turn on his heels—I'll sock him one in the jaw!"[17] No surprise, then, that Castorena should pummel would-be deserters with his carbine, threatening to "beat the Hell" out of those who ran, and be eager in his ire to do so.[18] One also finds the origin of Julia in Silvine, and the comparison between Napoleon III and Porfirio Díaz needs no comment. There are also the evocations of troops, crowds, mobs—the shouts, jostling, and massed brutishness for which Zola is well known, and which Frías also does masterfully well in painting the faceless hordes of *Tomochitecos* and anonymous Mexican troops; but as though to dispel all doubt as to *Tomochic's* origin, we have the final moments of both novels bearing striking similarity, with the protagonists gazing out over a burning city (Paris) or village (Tomochic), while black clouds of smoke darken the sky:

> Full of anguish, Jean turned away and looked at Paris. At that radiant end of a lovely Sunday the slanting sun, low on the horizon, cast over the huge

city a blazing red light. It might have been a sun of blood over a limitless sea. . . .

Then Jean felt an extraordinary sensation. It seemed to him, as day was slowly dying over this burning city, that a new dawn was already breaking. [. . .]

Still weeping, Jean said again:
"Good-bye!"[19]

And when he [Mercado] raised his head and straightened up, again resigned and strengthened, his tearful eyes, his sad eyes saw the darkness below stained by the fateful flames of the dead, burning in deep silence of the valley . . . and above, toward the east, over the crests of the hills, the dawn . . .

Then he shouted:
"Bugler, sound reveille!" (*Tomochic*, p. 149)

Adapting *Tomochic* after *La Débâcle* did not end Frías' debt to Zola; in fact, it only set a pattern that he followed thereafter. His earlier poems, published in the years after his military experience, show leanings toward a scientistic and often atheistic (though never amoral) viewpoint as they dwelt on vices and decadence. We have seen that in 1895 he wrote an extended poem entitled "Sara" which he published in *El Demócrata*. Accompanied by an article of Rubén M. Campos praising Frías and the triumph of Naturalism, the poem recounts the story of an innocent young man brought to ruin by Sara, a prostitute. It is really Zola's *Nana* in 441 lines of verse. Frías, at this time, was even using "Germinal" as his pseudonym in newspaper articles, after Zola's novel of that name.

But it was in his novels that he followed Zola most closely. Dedicated to truth and accuracy with fierce zeal, he saw the novel as an extension of journalistic reform. Yet Frías, like Zola (who was also a journalist), could not remain the detached and objective observer that Naturalism said one should be. Their novels hide no outrage, no indignation; nor are their characters the random, average subjects who appeared, in the novels of Flaubert, to govern themselves autonomously; they are unusual or exaggerated types who inexorably come to represent a vice, a virtue, a class, or a viewpoint. Everywhere the author's hand is apparent, guiding, molding, and twisting, in accordance with Frías' and Zola's ideas of how their characters should behave.

When Frías wrote *El amor de las sirenas*, with its detailed portraits of city life and its worst, he undoubtedly had Zola's *L'Assomoir* in mind. These passages in particular point up Frías' use of morbid detail couched in clinical terminology, which Frías for a time inherited from his French master:

> He felt his heart crushed by brutal hands; fatigue in his back; the stinging of innumerable, of millions of needles on his skin. . . . (*El amor de las sirenas*, p. 393)

> Thousands of pins stung him. There was a sort of weight all over his skin; a cold, wet beast dragged over his thighs and sunk its fangs into his flesh.[20]

Zola's skill in depicting the force and movement of a crowd is well known, and in many of his works, Frías achieves an identical effect. In the party scenes at the beginning of *El último duelo*, at the banquet of *¿Aguila o sol?*, during the sea outing and the various parties and gatherings in *El triunfo de Sancho Panza* and battle scenes of *Tomochic*, Frías evokes the sounds and colors, the energy and movement of groups, crowds, or mobs; often one catches bits of conversation, a face here or there, as though a person passed nearby, to be noticed for a second and quickly lost again in the mass. In *¿Aguila o sol?*, the scene of Mercado's inflammatory speech to the populace of Mixtlán is directly comparable to Étienne's address before the strikers in Zola's *Germinal*. There is the same crescendo of emotion in the crowd, the same interspersed shouts, and the same raucous uproar as the masses overflow with hate.

In fact, *¿Aguila o sol?* reveals other interesting points of comparison with *Germinal*, to the degree that once again it is apparent that Frías has adapted a work by Zola to his own use. Consider the plot: Mercado, like Éttienne, is an outsider whose arrival (in both cases after a life of frustration and failure) permits him to observe with curiosity and care the lifestyles and hardships of the local inhabitants, the intimacies of their daily dealings, and even something of their past history. Thus Frías paints a detailed picture of life in Mixtlán through Mercado's eyes, just as Zola portrayed the miners' lot as viewed by Étienne.

Identical problems exist in both communities, and the situation is not too subtle: landowners and industrial bourgeoisie own everything, while the workers and their families have nothing. Étienne, soon after his arrival, questions an old man and receives a detailed listing of mines, workers, production of coal, workshops, and factories, whereupon Étienne, his curiosity piqued, asks who all this belongs to, and the *ancien* replies: " 'Eh? Whose is it? Who knows?

People.' And with his hand he pointed out a vague place, an unknown and far-flung place, populated by those for whom the Mahue had dug in the vein for a century."[21]

Mercado's interview in ¿*Aguila o sol?* takes place in a tavern with the local barflies, who launch into a similar inventory of farms, mines, business firms, and such. Mercado makes his query:

"Whose mines are they?"
"Whose do you think? The Aguila family's and the gringos'. . . ."
"No," rectified Mezalitos. "They belong to the Mixtleca Industrial and Agricultural Company."
"It's all the same. Here everything is monopolized by the bourgeois bastards and the fat-cat traitors." (Pp. 246-47)

Following their respective periods of observation, investigation, and analysis, each protagonist embarks on a crusade and succeeds in arousing the people against their oppressors with his inflammatory speeches, thus setting in motion the wheels of revolution. In both cases, troops and a display of armed force are necessary to restore order among the angry masses, and the heros, both Étienne and Mercado, are forced to flee, Étienne following the failure of the miners' strike and Mercado after the riot caused by his sixteenth of September speech. But as they both depart and the novels end, they leave the clear impression that they have lit a fire that will not so easily be extinguished: ¿*Aguila o sol?* relates briefly the wave of unrest spreading across the Mexican republic, and *Germinal* more subtly shows Étienne walking across the fields, keenly aware of the miners below him who are awaiting their opportunity to burst forth again.

Laws of heredity, as they were understood to be at that time, form much of Zola's theoretical framework in his Rougon-Macquart series as each novel traces strengths and weaknesses from generation to generation. He and other cultivators of the Zolaesque Naturalism thus illustrated their understanding of Social Darwinism with the "scientific novel," usually with a generous sprinkling of vices and abnormalities. Zola's French dynasty, encompassing some twenty novels, found its Mexican echo in ¿*Aguila o sol?*, in which Frías passes all Mexico through the eye of a needle by means of the Aguila family, all in that single sprawling novel. While Zola's genealogical tree has three separate branches representing upper, middle, and lower classes, the Aguila family has only the wealthy and poorer factions. Throughout, both Frías and Zola attempt to symbolize their respective nations as families divided against themselves into haves and have nots, oppressors and oppressed.

Little wonder, then, that in both the Aguilas and the Rougon-Macquart line, the poorer sides of the families are illegitimate. Anticipating Octavio Paz' symbolic vision of a Mexico historically symbolized by *chingón* and *chingado*[22] (roughly the rapist and the raped), Frías' dynasty branched off when the first Mexican Aguila, a colonial tyrant, raped an Indian girl, Flor de Sol, and thus produced the outcaste lineage of the family from which descended generations of liberals and patriots, many of them journalists—all of them poor. Over the years they struggled against their oppressors, quite notably the rich and legitimate Aguilas. The poorer Aguilas traditionally embody vigor, wholesomeness, and the common sense virtues, whereas the rich side of the family shows a history of inherited and cultivated decadence. Now going rapidly downhill, the later generations are little more than bullies and thugs.

The great gulf between factions is drawn most clearly in the youngest members of this forked family tree. Gaudelia embodies all that is good; her energy, beauty, talent, and willingness to give of herself in service and sacrifice stand out in sharp contrast to Pepe León Aguila, a debauched and degenerate playboy who preaches shallow and half-digested maxims of Positivism. Here are the greater outlines of Zola's hereditary sketchbooks, but the reader will find no careful analysis, no psychological subtleties, as Frías paints with the bold colors of a cartoonist; but so, often did Zola. Both authors, while attempting to portray thier society with the jewelers' eye, fail to hide their own puritanical horror at the gruesome realities they have uncovered. In the final analysis they show themselves to be reformers, not objective scientists, and their indignation, disgust, even their despair, are altogether evident.

Zola's influence on Frías is, then, massive: Frías adapted Zola's works to his own uses from his first novel to his last, plus others in between; Zola's ideological framework became Frías' own, and Frías' style shows the mark of Zola as well. But there are differences, mainly qualitative ones. Zola planned and researched his monumental and wide-sweeping novels with a meticulousness for which Frías had little patience. At the core of Zola's ideology was the primordial "beast within" all men, while Frías' *bête noire* of Porfirianism was essentially exterior and other-imposed; it was an unjust system whereby evil men legally preyed upon the weak, and to ascribe such injustice wholly to genes, chromosomes, or "bad blood" would have denied the oppressors their guilt. This Frías could not do. Still, the similarities are undeniable, and in the really important task of prodding a complacent society, both Frías and Zola went about their business in much the same way.

IV *The Epic Urge*

The possibility that Frías displayed epic or near-epic stirrings has cropped up several times in this study, and the moment is now ripe to consider this idea. Difficult as it is, at first flance, to see Miguel Mercado's fitful and failure-bound sorties against the established order as even remotely comparable to deeds of Odysseus, Beowulf, or El Cid, the resemblance between some of Frías' works and the classical epic is undeniable there.

While no attempt to define the epic to total satisfaction can be made here, we can enumerate some elements generally held in connection with that genre. Central to an epic is an incident around which all action revolves and that a given nation, race, or tribe takes as having been particularly noteworthy in its history or heritage. It is usually an incident having to do with war. Key to the turn of events is a hero who typifies or represents his nation, race, or tribe. The style is elevated, events are described in great detail, and imagery, whether ornate or colloquial, reinforces national, racial, or tribal cultural characteristics. The story often begins at midpoint, and flashbacks later show events leading up to the central incident. The poet or author usually offers up at some point an invocation to the muse, a prayer for divine inspiration from some higher power, and elsewhere he takes care to pose an epic question that in some way summarizes the work's thematic thrust. Also, aid often comes from unexpected quarters (often divine or supernatural) to give guidance to the hero after a series of hardships and defeats.

It is most enlightening to consider all of Frías' Miguel Mercado novels *(Tomochic, Miserias de México, El triunfo de Sancho Panza,* and *¿Aguila o sol?)* as a single and incomplete epic. Broken down into these four divisions, they are as cantos. As the epic form dictates, the story line contains many episodes but is in itself simple. It commences with Mercado's trek to the mountains to do battle in Tomochic, but flashbacks in *Tomochic* and *Miserias de México* provide background to that drama in describing the events leading up to the campaign and also in filling in details of Mercado's early life. Taking *Tomochic* in itself, the massacre is the central incident, but the Miguel Mercado series *in toto* has as its pivotal incident the Mexican Revolution, beginning with revolts leading to Díaz' fall, the importance of which is still overpowering to the Mexican nation and the roots of which Frías traces (in ¿*Aguila o sol?*) directly to outrages typified in the Tomochic campaign some seventeen years before.

Certainly Frías had originally no such design in mind but, as we have seen often, his urges were characteristically directed toward the epic as though he were casting about for fertile heroic soil. Looking back, Frías/Mercado's participation in the shameful Tomochic campaign may be seen as the epic hero's classical fall from honor (as the Cid's), a stain that is both in and above the hero's life, because it represents Mexico's crimes against its people. Frías' ensuing atonement is a life left in disarray, a series of ignominies, exile from social and professional circles in *Miserias de México*, and out-and-out defeat in *El triunfo de Sancho Panza*. These are likewise ignominious for Mexico, as they serve to underscore in a highly personal way the rot and decay that pervaded Mexican life during those years and the disgraceful load of guilt his country had accumulated upon itself.

Standing at the end of his active career, Frías could begin to give shape, *a posteriori*, to his continuing epic. With ¿*Aguila o sol?*, design takes over where chance led before—or so it certainly appears. All of Frías' novels contain a form of the epic invocation by declaring, at one point or another, that the reader will there find "little art but much truth," in the manner that epic poets decried their own poor talent but depended on an outside source of inspiration—from the muses, God, or love, depending on the times. Frías appeals to truth as his guiding beacon and repeats it often. True to form, outside help comes to the hero of ¿*Aguila o sol?* in his hour of decision. It is not Diana or St. James, to be sure, but more earthbound and certainly more Mexican. It is Gaudelia Ramos, who stirs Mercado's flagging spirit and cajoles him into making the speech that kindles Mixtlán/Mexico into action against its oppressors. She, Frías takes care to explain, symbolizes the Mexican woman whose love and purity stand ready to redeem her people in times of need (pp. 311–12).

The supernatural element of classical epic could not be taken whole into Frías' epic, but the Dantean or Odyssan journey into the underworld can be sought and found in ¿*Aguila o sol?* and its hitherto unexplained dinner party in Mexico City at which the leading figures of the day are trundled forth, one by one. Actually, they are conjured up like the shades in Hades, as amidst the stench of cigar smoke and the clatter of glasses the reader meets José Juan Tablada, Amado Nervo, Carlos González Peña, Félix Díaz, José Gómez Ugarte, Angel de Campo, José Vasconcelos, Plutarco Elías Calles, José María Pino Suárez, Francisco Madero, Venustiano Carranza, Victoriano Huerta, and a host of others. Mercado records snatches of some figures' conversation while catching only a glimpse of others in the crowd, just long enough to take note of their presence there, as his epic forerunners had done in Hell or Hades. Here Pepe León Aguila speaks for Díaz, Satan himself, as he exalts: "Yes indeed, comrades; let us tell His Emperial Majesty Porfirio I to draw his sword and not leave it stilled . . . ; let him fight his enemies; let him exterminate the untruthful; let him clear the moats; let him throw overboard the ballast of the indigenous masses, who are but swarms of worms. . . . Thus spake Zarathustra and thus speak I. . ." (p. 197)

At this point Mercado also asks the epic question, which is the burning question at this moment of history's crucial juncture: it is, "What will become of Mexico?"

Fifteen years from now! . . . Remember, Miguel [he confides to himself], remember then, if perhaps you haven't kicked off in the hospital or if your companions of the press and your bosses and your friends haven't shot you. . . . You will see then who among all these will have drowned in the deluge and who will have saved themselves in the ark, and who will have saved or ruined Mexico. . . . Fifteen years from now. (pp. 207–208)

And so Frías' appearance in Mexico City to witness the unlikely aggregation of great, near-great, and truly mediocre personages of his day at their "fantasmo-historical" banquet is not so much an irritating or perplexing digression in ¿*Aguila o sol?*, if we see it as Mercado's obligatory descent to the nether regions to mingle with the restless spirits of the past, present, and future.

What, then, of Mercado as the epic hero? Circumstances imposed on him the distance from his peers and the task of defining himself as Mexico's Everyman, working toward some compromise between what he is and what he should be. Capable of failure, blunder, and aimlessness, while at the same time marking a zig-zag course toward destiny, Frías/Mercado bares the fibers of his soul in frank confession to a degree that is uncommon in Hispanic literature, most especially in Mexico. Thus his trials and travails become Mexico's own as the stumbling hero faces one outrage after another, himself tainted by the national vices of weakness and guilt. This is the Frías/Mercado who stood idly by as the *Tomochic* expedition became a turkey shoot, who later drowned a quixotic spirit in alcohol and self-pity, who sought foolishly to reform Mazatlán with a stroke of the pen and instead was run out of town like a common thief. (Epic figures are given to fits of stupidity.) Mercado/Frías is the Mexico that had to rid itself of a dictatorship that was sapping its vitality, but even more urgently needed to cleanse itself and find direction from within. The Mercado of ¿*Aguila o sol?* does just that with a clearness of spirit and a vision of victory that were taking form in him as they developed around him. Since the "fifteen years" of his epic question add up to approximately the writing and publication date of ¿*Aguila o sol?*, the epic question proved further prophetic as to Frías' death and that of the series, likely meant to carry Mercado through the Madero era, Huerta, the convention and its factional struggles, Carranza and Obregón, to final victory in future volumes left unwritten by his death.

While stylistically Frías' prose in its earthy pungence is frankly not of an epic nature, his language *is* directed to his people in their own vernacular, a style epic poets have also often employed, and in all respects breathes a nationality that is undeniable and a martial emphasis that would do credit, at moments, to Roland or the Cid.

Whether this piling on of epic style and structure was accidental or not is unprovable, but the weight of evidence makes a believable case for a supposition that Frías was aware of the epic tendency and cultivated it, however sporadically, in earlier autobiographical works. Later, the historical and personal fact of the Mexican Revolution, seen retrospectively from the 1920s, was then delivered up to Frías as though made to order. His epic vision was redeemed and he (in a truly Odyssan transport of ego-fulfillment) set about bringing Mercado to his national triumph in seeking, as epic writers will, "to adapt the heroic ideal to unheroic times and to proclaim . . . a new concept of man's grandeur and nobility."[23] But the epic of Miguel Mercado was never finished.

Notes and References

Chapter One

1. Francisco I. Madero, *La sucesión presidencial en 1910*, 3rd ed. (Mexico City: Bouret, 1911), pp. 198–99.
2. Daniel Cosío Villegas, *Historia moderna de México* (Mexico City: Ed. Hermes, 1955), I, 767–925.
3. Ibid. IV xvi–xvii.
4. Leopoldo Zea, *El positivismo en México* (Mexico City: Colegio de México, 1943–1944), p. 59.
5. Ibid., pp. 44–74.
6. Ibid., pp. 74–76.
7. Cosío Villegas, IV, 609.
8. See Ibid. IV Parte Primera.
9. See especially, Jesús Silva Herzog, *Breve historia de la Revolución Mexicana*, Vol. 8 (Mexico City: Fondo de Cultura Económica, 1965), I, 38.
10. Cosío Villegas, IV, 415–25.
11. Ibid., IV, pp. 52–82.
12. *El triunfo de Sancho Panza* (Mexico City: Herrera, 1911), pp. 75–76. Frías' novels, especially *Miserias de México* (Mexico City: Botas, 1916), provide much biographical information on Frías and have been used by Delfina Grace and David López Peimbert (see bibliography). However, the information in these sources is neither dependable nor complete, as interviews and letters with the author's widow, now deceased, have shown.
13. *¿Aguila o sol?* (Mexico City: Impr. Franco-Mexicana, 1923), pp. 225–26.
14. *Triunfo*, pp. 75–83; "El poetastro de 'los pericos,' " *El Demócrata*, June 12, 1895, p. 2.
15. *Triunfo*, pp. 83–86.
16. Letter to the author dated September 13, 1965. José Valades, a noted historian and diplomat, knew Heriberto Frías intimately in Mazatlán.
17. *Triunfo*, p. 88.
18. "Escritores contemporáneos: Heriberto Frías," *Biblos*, November 22, 1919, p. 1.

19. The three hundred-odd inhabitants had risen up in the name of Teresa Urrea, the "Saint of Cabora," who was reputed to possess miraculous powers. See Mario Gill, "Teresa Urrea, la Santa de Cabora," *Historia Mexicana*, 4, no. 4 (1956-1957), 626-44. This article gives a complete accounting of events leading up to the campaign and of the campaign itself.

20. Frías calls her Lola in *Miserias de México*, but the records of the ensuing court martial reveal her name as that given here. See David López Peimbert's thesis *Tomochic* (Mexico City: University of Mexico, 1963), p. 116.

21. López Peimbert, pp. 104-105. This sort of thing was not unusual in the life of *El Demócrata* or its editors either. See José C. Valadés, *El porfirismo: historia de un regimen* (Mexico City: Ed. Patria, 1948), I, 45-46.

22. López Peimbert, p. 123.

23. *Triunfo*, p. 137.

24. *Miserias*, pp. 5-6.

25. *Gil Blas*, March 20, 1895, p. 1.

26. *Tomochic* (Rio Grande City, Texas: Imprenta de Jesús T. Recio, 1894).

27. *Miserias*, pp. 17-18.

28. Ibid., p. 15.

29. "Naufragio," *El Demócrata*, June 20-November 7, 1895; *El amor de las sirenas: "Los destripados"* (Mazatlán: Valadés, 1908).

30. See Manuel Mañón, *Historia del Teatro Principal de México* (Mexico City: Editorial Cultura, 1932). pp. 162-73.

31. *El último duelo* (Mexico City: Imprenta de la Revista Militar, 1896).

32. From an open letter by Frías, "El señor Fernando Iglesias falta a la verdad: carta al mismo historiógrafo," *México Nuevo*, June 1, 1910, p. 4.

33. *Tomochic* (Barcelona: Maucci, 1899). For a fuller accounting of Frías' numerous articles and lesser known works, the reader is referred to the author's "Bibliografía de Heriberto Frías," *Boletín Bibliográfico de la Secretaría de Hacienda y Crédito Público*, 463 (July 1, 1971), 26-32.

34. Though called "Fina" in *Miserias de México*, her name was that given here. (Letter from Aurea Frías to the author dated November 11, 1965.)

35. *Biblioteca del niño mexicano* (Barcelona: Maucci, 1900).

36. *Episodios militares mexicanos*, 2 vols. (Paris: Bouret, 1901).

37. *El general Félix Díaz* (Mexico City: El Progreso Industrial, 1901).

38. Angel María Garabay, ed., *Diccionario de biografía, geografía e historia de México* (Mexico City: Porrúa, 1964), p. 563; María Elena Allera de Morris, "Heriberto Frías" (Dissertation, University of Mexico, 1951), p. 18.

39. It may be slightly misleading to characterize *género chico* as vaudeville, but the differences are slight. *Género chico* centered around one act musical farces laden with satires and more or less off-color humor.

40. See José C. Valadés, *Mis confesiones* (Mexico City: Editoriales Mexicanos Unidos, 1967), pp. 117 ff.

41. *Tomochic* (Mazatlán: Valadés, 1906).
42. "Escritores contemporáneos," p. 2; Andrés Magallón, in a letter to the author dated August 21, 1965; Valadés *El porfirismo*, p. 157.
43. "¿Cuál es el estado que sufre más ignominias? Abriremos un concurso para averiguarlo," *El Constitucional*, October 29, 1910, p. 1.
44. *El Constitucional*, April 7, 1910, p. 3.
45. September 15, 1910, p. 1.
46. *El Constitucional*, August 4, 1910, p. 1.
47. *El Constitucional*, August 10, 1910, p. 2.
48. *El Constitucional*, October 7, 1910, p. 1.
49. *El Constitucional*, October 5, 1910, p. 1.
50. *El Constitucional*, October 15, 1910, p. 1.
51. *El Constitucional*, October 25, 1910, p. 1. Bulnes was one of the original *científicos*.
52. *Los piratas del boulerand* (Mexico City: Botas, n.d). Juan Iguíniz, in his *Bibliografía de novelistas mexicanos*, estimated its publication date as 1916 and subsequent bibliographers have accepted this, but as *Los piratas* was advertised for sale in the office of *La Convención* in the spring of 1915, this latter date seems more accurate.
53. Ibid., p. 96.
54. *El Constitucional*, October 29, 1910, p. 1.
55. *Tomochic* (Paris: Bouret, 1911).
56. *El Constitucional*, October 31, 1910, p. 1.
57. Interview with the author, August 23, 1966.
58. *El Constitucional*, November 10, 1910, p. 1.
59. *El Constitucional*, November 10, 1910, p. 1.
60. *El Constitucional*, November 11, 1910, p. 1.
61. *El Demócrata*, May 2, 1934, n. p.
62. Silva Herzog, II, 32–35; *El Demócrata*, November 9, 1915, p. 6. In the latter article, Frías intimated that he and Carranza were good friends at that time.
63. *La Convención*, December 18, 1914, p. 2.
64. *La Convención*, December 19, 1914, p. 2. *El Plan de Ayala* (Declaration at Ayala) was Zapata's call to arms; it was a platform centered around agrarian reform.
65. See Robert E. Quirk, *The Mexican Revolution 1914–1915: The Convention of Aguascalientes* (New York: The Citadel Press, 1963).
66. Letters to the author from Aurea Frías, November 11, 1965, and January 7, 1967; *El Demócrata*, November 9, 1915, pp. 1–6.
67. *La vida de Juan Saldado* (Mexico City: Imprenta Franco-Americana, 1918).
68. Author's interview with Mrs. Frías, August 23, 1966.
69. *Album histórico popular de la Cuidad de Mexico* (Mexico City: Soria, 1925).

70. *El Universal*, November 14, 1925, Sect. 1, p. 4.
71. *¿Aguila o sol?*, p. 314.

Chapter Two

1. Frías used two spellings, Tomóchic and Tomochic, in referring to the village and his novel. For uniformity's sake I choose the latter, since that is the current usage and since Frías favored it in later writings.
2. Mariano Azuela, *Cien años de novela mexicana* (Mexico City: Botas, 1947), p. 218; René Avilés, "Heriberto Frías y la moderna novela mexicana," *Suma Bibliográfica* 4, 11–12 (1948), 318–20; "Escritores contemporáneos," pp. 1–2; E. R. Moore, "Heriberto Frías and the Novel of the Mexican Revolution," *Modern Language Forum*, xxvii, no. 1 (1942), 18.
3. For further details regarding the Tomochic campaign, particularly its causes, see Gill, pp. 626–44.
4. First ed., *Ed Demócrata*, March 22, 1893, p. 1.
5. March 14, 1893, p. 2.
6. March 23, 1893, p. 1.
7. April 13, 1893, p. 1.
8. I am indebted to Professor Lawrens B. Perry and Mr. Richard F. Phillips of the Universidad de las Américas for searching out and decoding Díaz' telegrams from the Colección General Porfirio Díaz, kept on microfilm at the Universidad de las Américas. The following notes will refer to that collection.
9. "Telegramas," Roll 325, Documents 2172–74 (April 15, 1893).
10. "Telegramas," Roll 325, Documents 2201–41 (April 17, 1893); 2254–81 (April 18, 1893); 2301–09 (April 19, 1893); 2335–46 (April 20, 1893); 2333–2342 (April 20, 1893); 5622 (April 21, 1893); 2373–82 (April 21, 1893); 2586–2633 (April 27, 1893); 6059 (May 4, 1893); 6060 (Mat 4, 1893).
11. The court martial's transcript is reproduced in López Peimbert, pp. 93–125.
12. "Telegramas," Roll 325, Documents 2333–2342 (April 20, 1893); 5622 (April 21, 1893).
13. "Telegramas," Roll 325, Document 2343 (April 20, 1893). Italics mine.
14. *El Demócrata*, April 2, 1893, p. 1.
15. López Peimbert, p. 36.
16. *Tomochic*, 1968 ed., p. 10. This statement appeared for the first time in the fourth (1906) edition. All subsequent quotes from *Tomochic* will be from the 1968 edition unless otherwise noted.
17. Ibid., 14. Added to 4th ed.
18. Ibid., 135. New in the 4th ed. Teresa Urrea became known as the Saint of Cabora among Northern mountaineers when as a child she revived from an epileptic fit and her father proclaimed her miraculously resurrected. Both she and the amulets her father sold (mentioned in *Tomochic*,

p. 144) reputedly held life-giving powers. As she grew older she began to lead attacks against the government and to inspire revolt against Díaz in the name of God. Tomochic was only one of several communities that carried her banner. See Gill, 626–30.

19. *Tomochic*, 79. New in 3rd ed.
20. Ibid., 26. New in 4th ed.
21. Ibid., 136. New in 4th ed.
22. Ibid., 142. New in 4th ed.
23. J. Lloyd Read, *The Mexican Historical Novel: 1826–1910* (New York: Instituto de las Españas de los Estados Unidos, 1939), p. 280. His bibliography (p. 332) lists only the 1899 edition.
24. José Ferrel, "La novela nacional," prologue to *Tomochic*, 1906 and 1911 ed., p. 6.
25. Azuela, p. 219.

Chapter Three

1. The back cover of *El último duelo* of 1907 advertises an unpublished novel, "Los corsarios de la prensa" ("The Corsairs of the Press"), which may well have been the manuscript in question.
2. *El amor de las sirenas*, Introduction, n. p.
3. A pseudonym of Manuel Gutiérrez Nájera (1859–1895) Mexican poet and prose writer.
4. *El último duelo*, (Mexico City: Impr. y Casa Editorial de Valadés, 1907) Introduction, p. iii.
5. See Cosío Villegas, IV, 429.
6. This was actually *El Correo de la Tarde*. See *Triunfo*, ch. I.
7. A reference to Don Quixote, who called himself the "ingenious Knight of the Sorrowful Countenance."
8. Such an attitude calls to mind José Vasconcelos' view of racial determinism as set forth in his *Raza Cósmica (Cosmic Race)*, 1925.
9. Jorge Isaacs (1837–1895), Columbian author of the Romantic novel *María;* Gustavo Adolfo Bécquer (1836–1870), Spanish Romantic poet best known for his *Rimas (Rhymes);* Manuel Flores (1840–1885), Mexican Romantic poet of *Pasionarias (Passion Flowers)*.
10. See John S. Brushwood's "Heriberto Frías on Social Behavior and Redemptive Woman," *Hispania*, 45, 2 (May 1962), 249–53.
11. Ferrel, p. 6.
12. See Petronius, "Cena Trimalchionis," *Satiricon;* Horace, Satire II, 8; Juvenal, *Satires* V, XI.
13. *Tomochic* in all eds.; p. 140 in 1968 ed.
14. The 1911 edition, as we have seen, contained no changes of text.
15. López Peimbert, p. 72.
16. Avilés p. 320.
17. See especially *Miserias*, pp. 12–15.

Chapter Four

1. Not to be confused with his novel of the same title.
2. *Leyendas históricas mexicanas* (Mexico City: Editora Naciònal, 1957), p. 5.
3. Mariano Picón-Salas, *De la conquista a la independencia*, 4th ed. (Mexico City: Fondo de Cultura Económica, 1965), p. 30.
4. Among Indianist authors in other countries were Juan León Mera (Equador), Manuel de Jesús Galván (Dominican Republic), Clorinda Matto de Turner (Peru), José Joaquín Pérez (Dominican Republic), Juan Zorrilla de San Martín (Uruguay), and Lucio Victoriano Mansilla (Argentina). Among the few Mexican examples of Indianist literature from that period are Ireneo Paz' *Doña Marina* and Eulogio Palma y Palma's *La hija de Tutul-xiu*.
5. Ciro B. Ceballos, *En Turánia* (Mexico City: Tipografía Ecomómica, 1902), p. 134.
6. Read, pp. 289–90.
7. Ibid., p. 287.
8. *Episodios*, "La toma de Granaditas," ("The Taking of Granaditas"), I, 30–43, "El ataque de San Diego" ("The Attack at San Diego"), I, 181–94.
9. The copies used in this study were loaned to the author by John S. Brushwood.
10. *El fin de un heroe azteca, o la eterna maldición (The End of an Aztec Hero, or Eternal Perdition)*, 3rd series, p. 5.
11. *Once años de guerra (Eleven Years of War)*. 4th series, p. 15.
12. Henry Bamford Parkes, *A History of Mexico*, 3rd ed. (Boston: Houghton Mifflin Co., 1960), p. 282.
13. (Mexico City: El Progreso Industrial, 1901). The University of Texas Latin American Collection possesses the only copy of this work that I have located, either in Mexico or elsewhere.
14. The only copy of *Juan Soldado* that I have located is in the Pedro Robredo Collection of the Instituto Tecnológico y de Estudios Superiores de Monterrey, Nuevo León, Mexico.
15. A largely guerrilla-fought civil war of 1858–1861, waged over the passage of Mexico's reformist constitution of 1857. It was also known as the war of the Reform.
16. José Guadalupe Posada, 1851–1913, artist of satirical caricatures and engravings.
17. Frías' version of "Juan Soldado" is not the better known one found in *corridos* or popular ballads about an executed deserter from the army. See Merle E. Simmons, *The Mexican CORRIDO as a Source for Interpretive Study of Modern Mexico (1870–1950)*, (Bloomington: Indiana University Press, 1957), p. 51.
18. Pages unnumbered.

19. The only extant copy I have located is in the Pedro Robredo Collection of the Instituto Technológico of Monterrey.
20. Overestimation of the scholarly leanings of the "popular classes" was not confined at that time to Frías. José Vasconcelos, when assuming the post of minister of education, is said to have ordered translations of Plato for general distribution as elementary reading primers!
21. Regarding exact dating of this work, see note 52, chapter 1.
22. These stories are found, respectively, in *El Imparcial*, 1897–1898; *El Demócrata*, 1895; *El Constitucional*, 1909; and *Miserias de Mexico*, pp. 75–132. Note again that Frías' novel *Miserias de México* should not be confused with the articles of the same name published in *El Constitucional*.
23. "Miserias de México: El bautismo de sangre," *El Constitucional*, September 29, 1910, p. 4.
24. "La virgen sabia y fuerte" ("The Wise and Strong Virgin"), *El Constitucional*, April 19, 1910, p. 4.
25. "El alma en pena" ("The Ghost"), *Miserias de México*, p. 87. A *chinampa* is a garden tract among the "floating gardens" of Mexico's central valley.
26. "El bautismo de sangre," p. 4.
27. "Un tigre viejo," ("An Old Tiger"), *Miserias de México*, p. 100.
28. "Las perlas" ("The Pearls"), p. 97.
29. "Don Isabel," *El Imparcial*, August 20, 1898.
30. "Un escándalo grave" ("A Serious Scandal"), *El Constitucional*, October 1, 1910, p. 4.
31. *La Revista Moderna*, vol. 3 (1900), pp. 98–101 and pp. 10–11, respectively. Regarding the first title, the reader may already know that in Mexican dialect, *almuerzo* can mean breakfast and not lunch as in standard Spanish.
32. This story was incorporated without change into the 1906 and later editions of the novel *Tomochic* as Chapter 31.
33. "Tu beso," *El Mundo Ilustrado*, June 7, 1896, p. 358.
34. "Pecadora en sueños," *El Mundo Ilustrado*, September 6, 1896, p. 151.
35. In mythology, a dark world between earth and hell.
36. *El Demócrata*, December 15, 1895, pp. 1–2. The poem is dated 1892.
37. *El Demócrata*, December 22, 1895, p. 1.
38. From the papers of Aurea Frías.
39. Failure to find any mention of Frías' plays in newspapers or in histories of the Mexican theater leads me to believe that they were hardly major events.

Chapter Five

1. José Joaquín Fernández de Lizardi (1776–1827), author of *El*

Periquillo Sarniento (The Itching Parrot); and Mariano Azuela (1873–1952), best known for his novel *Los de abajo (The Underdogs).*

2. René Wellek and Austin Warren, *Theory of Literature*, 3rd ed., (New York: Harcourt, Brace & World, 1956) p. 216.

3. Only two examples among many studies of the novel of the Mexican Revolution are Antonio Magaña Esquivel, *La novela de la Revolución (The Novel of the Revolution)*, vol. 1 (Mexico City: Biblioteca del Instituto Nacional de Estudios Históricos de la Revolución Mexicana, 1964); and Adalbert Dessau, *La novela de la Revolución Mexicana (The Novel of the Mexican Revolution)* (Mexico City: Fondo de Cultura Económica, 1972).

4. R. Anthony Castagnaro, *The Early Spanish American Novel* (New York: Las Americas, 1971), p. 65.

5. Carlton Beals, *Mexican Maze* (Philadelphia: Lippincott, 1931), p. 276; Castagnaro, p. 65.

6. Azuela, *Cien años*, pp. 209–10.

7. *Tomochic*, p. 43.

8. *El Constitucional*, October 15, 1910, p. 1.

9. *El Constitucional*, November 10, 1910, p. 1.

10. *La Convención*, December 16, 1914, p. 2.

11. *Album Histórico Popular*, pp. 9, 28.

12. *El amor de las sirenas*, p. 91.

13. *La Convención*, December 18, 1914, p. 2.

14. The hope of cultural and racial fusion in producing in Latin America a new "hybrid" civilization found voice in José Enrique Rodo's *Ariel* (1900), Ricardo Rojas' *La restauración nacionalista (The Nationalistic Restoration,* 1909), and José Vasconcelos' *La raza cósmica (The Cosmic Race,* 1925).

15. John Rutherford, *Mexican Society during the Revolution: A Literary Approach* (Oxford: Clarendon Press, 1971), p. 82.

16. Emile Zola, *The Debacle*, trans. by L. W. Tancock (Harmondsworth: Penguin Classics, 1972).

17. *The Debacle*, p. 257.

18. *Tomochic*, p. 63.

19. *The Debacle*, pp. 508–509.

20. Emile Zola, *L'Assomoir* (Paris: G. Charpentier, 1930), pp. 258–59.

21. Emile Zola, *Germinal* (Paris: G. Charpentier, 1928), I, 10–11.

22. Octavio Paz, *The Labyrinth of Solitude: Life and Thought in Mexico*, tr. by Lysander Kemp (New York: Grove Press, Inc., 1961), pp. 74–88.

23. C. M. Bowra, "Some Characteristics of Literary Epic," *A Grammar of Literary Criticism, Concepts and Aims*, ed. Lawrence Sargent Hall (New York: Macmillan, 1965), p. 3.

Selected Bibliography

PRIMARY SOURCES

The reader who wishes a more complete bibliography of Frías' works is referred to J. W. Brown's "Bibliografía de Heriberto Frías" (see Secondary Sources). In the brief listing below only the better known and accessible works are included. In the case of multiple publications, only the most recent will be shown, with the year of first publication immediately after the title.

1. Novels

¿Aguila o sol? Novela histórica mexicana. Mexico City: Imprenta Franco-Mexicana, 1923.
El amor de las sirenas: "Los destripados." Mazatlán: Valadés, 1908.
El triunfo de Sancho Panza: Novela de crítica social mexicana. Mexico City: Imprenta de Luis Herrera, 1911.
El Último duelo: Un crimen social de la época del presidente Manuel González, 1896. 2nd ed. Mexico City: Imprenta y Casa Editorial de Valadés, 1907.
Miserias de México. México City: Botas, 1916.
Tomochic. 1893. 6th ed. with prologue and notes by James W. Brown. Mexico City: Porrúa, 1968.

2. Historical Works

Episodios militares mexicanos. 1901. 2 vol. Mexico City: Editora Nacional, 1955.
Leyendas históricas mexicanas. 1899. Mexico City: Editora Nacional, 1957.

3. Contemporary Satires

"Cáscaras y semillas," in *Miserias de México,* pp. 75–132. Mexico City: Botas, 1916.
Los Piratas del boulevard. Mexico City: Botas, n.d. [1915?].

SECONDARY SOURCES

AVILÉS, RENÉ. "Heriberto Frías y la moderna novela mexicana." *Suma Bibliográfica*, IV, 11–12 (1948), 318–20. Sees *Tomochic* as a precursor of later Mexican Realism.

AZUELA, MARIANO. *Cien años de novela mexicana*. Mexico: Botas, 1947. Pp. 209–25. *Tomochic* measures up to Azuela's very particular yardstick of Mexican Realism.

BROWN, JAMES W. "Bibliografia de Heriberto Frías." *Boletín Bibliográfico de la Secretaría de Hacienda y Crédito Público*, 463 (1971), 26–32. Contains a listing of some four hundred works by Frías.

———. "Heriberto Frías, A Mexican Zola." *Hispania*, L, 3 (September 1967), 467–71. Points up Zola's influence upon Frías.

BRUSHWOOD, JOHN S. "Heriberto Frías on Social Behavior and Redemptive Woman." *Hispania*, XLV, 2 (May 1962), 249–53. Shows Frías' search for basic human values in a superficial society.

LÓPEZ PEIMBERT, DAVID. "Tomóchic." Thesis, Universidad Nacional Autónoma de México, 1963. Paints Frías as a revolutionary.

MAGAÑA ESQUIVEL, ANTONIO. "Heriberto Frías, precursor." *La novela de la Revolución*, I, 53–60. Mexico: Biblioteca del Instituto Nacional de Estudios Históricos de la Revolución Mexicana, 1964. Brief summary of Frías' life and works.

MOORE, E. R. "Heriberto Frías and the Novel of the Mexican Revolution." *Modern Language Forum*, XXVII, 1 (1942), 12–27. Argues convincingly that Frías saw through the complacency of his times.

Index

(The works of Frías are listed under his name)

Ahumada, Miguel, 21, 22, 41, 42, 43
Atheneum of Youth (Ateneo de la Juventud), 111, 112
Azuela, Mariano: *The Underdogs (Los de abajo)* and others, 39, 49, 51, 52, 54, 57, 71, 100–104, 112, 133

Barreda, Gabino. See Positivism
Beals, Carlton: *Mexican Maze*, 102

Cabora, The Saint of (Teresa Urrea), 45, 125, 127–28
Carranza, Venustiano, 33, 34, 35, 36, 122, 123, 126
Chávez, Cruz, 39, 41, 44, 51
Chihuahua, state of, 20, 21, 22, 41, 43, 44
Clausell, Joaquín, 21, 22, 41, 42, 43, 44
Compte, August. See Positivism
Concha, Adalberto, 43
Costumbrismo, 47, 53, 73, 76

Díaz, Félix. See *General Félix Díaz* under Frías' works
Díaz, Porfirio, 13–17, 22, 24, 27, 28, 29, 30, 31, 40, 41, 42, 43, 44, 45, 65, 66, 67, 79, 83, 85, 86, 87, 89, 99, 101, 103, 104, 105, 108, 109, 112

Epic, 48, 54, 64, 97–98, 120–23

Fernández de Lizardi, José Joaquin: *The Itching parrot (El periquillo sarniento)*, 13, 89, 100, 103
Ferrel, José, 52, 69, 87
Frías, Antonia Figueroa de, 24–26, 28
Frías, Aurea Delgado de, 26, 31, 32, 35, 36, 37
Frías, Heriberto: as a revolutionary, 39–45, 105–106; attends National Military Academy, 19; attends National Preparatory School, 18; during postrevolutionary years, 36–37; in Chihuahua, 22; in Mexican Revolution, 32–36; in Mexico City, 22–26, 27–31; in military service, 19–22, 25, 40–45; style, 69–73
WORKS–DRAMA:
"Cayman, The" ("El caimán"), 26, 98–99
"Interlude" ("Zarzuela"), 26, 98
WORKS–POETRY:
"Assault" ("Asalto"), 97
"At last fierce Hamlet" ("Resolución"), 98
"Sara," 97
"Your Kiss" ("Tu beso"), 95
WORKS–PROSE:
"The Breakfast" ("El almuerzo"), 94
"The Deluge in Mexico" ("El diluvio en México"), 34–35, 36
Derelict (Naufragio). See *The Love of Sirens*.
"Dogs of Tomochic, The" ("Los perros de Tomochic"), 47, 94
General Félix Díaz (El General Félix Díaz), 25, 85, 122
Heads or Tails? (¿Aguila o sol?), 36, 37, 52, 64–67, 68, 69, 71, 74, 81, 91, 98, 101–103, 104, 105, 107, 108, 112, 113, 117–19, 120, 121–22, 123
Last Duel, The (El último duelo), 24, 55, 59–61, 68, 117
Life of Juan the Soldier, The (La vida de Juan Soldado), 36, 49, 71, 75, 87–88, 107
Love of Sirens, The (El amor de las sirenas), 24, 35, 55, 56–59, 67, 68,

135

69, 106, 108, 109, 111, 116–17
Mexican Child's Library, The (La biblioteca del niño mexicano), 25, 49, 84–85, 87
Mexican Historical Legends (Leyendas históricas mexicanas), 75, 76–81, 85
Mexican Military Episodes (Episodios militares mexicanos), 25, 31, 49, 75, 81–84, 85, 87
Miseries of Mexico (Miserias de México), 23, 55, 62–64, 67, 68, 81, 106, 108, 111, 112, 120, 121
Pirates of the Boulevard, The (Los piratas del boulevard), 31, 34, 52, 71, 75, 90–92, 93, 94, 106
Popular Historical Album of Mexico City (Album histórico *popular de la Ciudad de México*), 37, 88–90
Tomochic, 13, 22, 23, 27, 31, 35, 38–54, 55, 62, 67–68, 72, 73–74, 75, 80, 81, 90, 101, 102, 104, 105, 106, 108, 114–16, 117, 120–21, 123
Triumph of Sancho Panza, The (El triunfo de Sancho Panza), 26, 31, 35, 61–62, 67, 68, 69, 106, 111, 117, 120, 121
González, Manuel, 59, 60

Huerta, Victoriano, 33, 122, 123

Impressionism in art, 73

Juárez, Benito, 14–15, 88

Lerdo de Tejada, 14, 17
Limantour, José Ives. See Positivism
López Peimbert, David, 44, 52, 124, 133

Madero, Francisco I., 13, 27, 31, 32, 33, 66, 105, 111, 112, 122, 123
Martínez, Rafael, 28, 36, 89
Mexican Revolution 28–36, 39–41, 43, 44, 46, 64, 67, 68, 84, 103, 105–106, 108, 123
Modernism, 58, 75, 79–80, 91–92, 96, 97
Moheno, Querido, 43
Montejo, Concepción, 21, 42
Monterde, Francisco, 103
Moore, Earnest R., 39, 103, 133

National Military Academy, The, 18, 19
National Preparatory School, The, 15, 16, 17, 18
Naturalism, 97, 113–120
Novel of the Mexican Revolution, 100–104, 112

Obregón, Alvaro, 33, 36, 108, 123

Palma, Ricardo, 78–79
Paz, Octavio, 119
Picón-Salas, Mariano, 78
Posada, Guadalupe, 87
Positivism: and August Compte, 14–15; and Barreda, 14–15, 110; and Frías, 104–113, 119; and Limantour, 15–16; and Naturalism, 113; and the *científicos*, 30, 105, 109; in Mexico, 13–17, 66, 70
Prieto, Guillermo, 19

Rangel, Gen. José María, 21, 22, 40, 42, 43
Read, J.L., 50, 79, 80
Realism, 70, 71, 87, 94, 102
Romanticism, 51, 52, 53, 70, 73, 80, 87, 96–97, 114
Rutherford, John, 111

Saint of Cabora, The. See Cabora, Saint of
Sierra, Justo, 25–26, 28–29, 87, 91–92, 95, 104

Tomochic (town of), 20–21, 38–39, 45, 48, 50, 64, 94–95, 104, 112, 115, 120–21, 123, 127
"Traditions." See Palma, Ricardo.

Urrea, Teresa. See Cabora, Saint of

Valadés, Andrés, 26, 50
Valadés, José, 20, 26, 124
Vasconcelos, José, 108, 111, 122, 130
Villa, Francisco, 33, 34, 35

Zola, Emile, 70, 97

THE LIBRARY
ST. MARY'S COLLEGE OF MARYLAND
ST. MARY'S CITY, MARYLAND 20686

085228